The Nomads Trilogy

Books 1, 2 & 3

Carol Bergman

The Nomads Trilogy
Books 1, 2 & 3

mediacs@gmail.com
(646) 216-9246

A Mediacs Publication

MEDIACS

CONTENTS

for the next generation

Henry, Javi, Carla, Ella, Harvey, Noah, Dylan, Wesley, Thea, Zoe, Ridley, Luca x2, Cora, Ellis, Marcela, Pearl Rose and Mila

> *may they grow up in a kinder,*
> *safer and more peaceful world*

A NOTE FROM THE AUTHOR

I do not know which of us has written this page.
—Jorge Luis Borges

The idea of a finished picture is a fiction.
—Barnett Newman

This is an unfinished work of fiction. The "I" in some of the stories is not the author, or it may resemble the author. The narrative persona may be a woman, or it may be a man, or it may be a person of indeterminate gender and age, or an omniscient reporter who knows everything, or nothing. Usually nothing.

Words resonate as we read, they become ours. Thank you, dear reader, for your collaboration. Together, we will create and recreate "Nomads."

NOMADS 1

Roma

3

Teresa was waiting at the bus stop with her friend. It was a hot day and they were both wearing big straw hats and sun glasses. Teresa was elegant, dressed in black trousers and a bolero jacket with sparkles, despite the hot day, and she was tall and as spindly as a crane. Lucy was tall too though stooped now, and she was still able to walk without a cane, but had trouble seeing.

The bus came and Teresa said, it's too crowded, let's wait for the next one, but Lucy wanted to get on. So they tried to get on. I wish people would realize I'm 100 years old, Teresa said, very loudly, but no one was listening, except for Lucy. She was younger, but not by much. These two were old friends and they were looking after each other and making friends all over the city, mostly on the buses going here and there. Oh bless her, bless her someone on line mumbled. It was moving slowly, too slowly for Teresa. She started shouting to the driver who was very busy helping a tourist get her metro card into the slot. Hey driver let us on, my friend is 100 years old, Lucy said. Did she get a card from the President? the driver asked. And Lucy said, I have it right here in my bag, driver. I carry all of Teresa's documents right here in this bag. So the driver announced that Teresa had preference, he was going to get her onto his bus. She had a cane, she was a 100 years old, born in 1914, and can we imagine how long ago that was, his schedule could wait, he would explain to his supervisor that he had stopped to take a venerable New Yorker on board and that was that.

What was that? Teresa asked. I'm a bit hard of hearing, you'll give us preference, let us jump this line? I've just been to the doctor and she took some wax out of my ears. You ever had that done? It's painful let me tell you.

Suddenly everyone's hurry was suspended. The bus sighed and idled and everyone was listening to Teresa talking to the driver. Sit near me, Madam, he said. I want some of your good genes to rub off on me.

A young woman sat on a bench in the conservatory garden. It was a cloudy day, but still warm, nearly October, and the leaves were turning. She was over-dressed and she was sad. Three girls in black strapless gowns walked past. They were holding bouquets of white lilies which surely were out of season, the young woman thought. She got up and walked towards the back of the garden which was dank and chilly, hoping to find relief from the heat of the day, but a bride and groom were underneath a tree posing for pictures. The photographer ordered them to smile.

There was a pond with plantings and the young woman settled on a bench facing the pond, and opened her book and began to read. A small blonde-haired boy came up to her and asked a question, but he spoke in a language she didn't understand. What he said was: *I am happy to be here.*

Although my bank is a global bank and has changed names twice in the last two years and has changed its color coordinated decor (it now has green lollipops) twice in the last two years, I still consider it my neighborhood bank which is ridiculous because I now live all the way uptown. That said, I am still in my old 'hood many days to shop and swim, meet clients or friends, and bank. And the reason I still consider this bank my neighborhood bank is because of Toshiba. She's a teller and she always smiles as I come up to the counter and asks how I am and I ask how she is. Most importantly, her name has significance because I didn't believe her nametag at first and thought maybe it was some kind of product placement the bank had organized for TOSHIBA, the computer company, if in fact it still exists with all the mergers and such these days. But sure enough, Toshiba is Toshiba's name. How did you get this name? I asked her one day. Meaning, what on earth were your parents thinking? They liked it, she said, and so did my grandmother who rules our family. We're from Guyana, a little village, you won't have heard of it, she said. And then one day I called her Toyota by mistake, but because Toshiba is so good natured, she didn't mind. I realized the *faux pas* as I was leaving the counter and turned back immediately. I can't believe I just called you Toyota, I said, I really apologize. Many people do that, she said. Then the next time I went to deposit a check, she wasn't there, and I was disappointed, but the time after that she was back from her holiday in Guyana and when I asked her how it was she said that her grandmother was failing, she was very frail, and she made her promise that if she ever had a son, she would call him SONY.

SHEEP MEADOW

Though it has been raining for several days and the sky is lowering even at mid-day, we decide to meet at the Sheep Meadow Café with its black rod-iron tables where people sit for hours and read or talk and dogs lie underfoot and the steel drums play. The wind swirls and pulls the over-sized green umbrellas out of their wooden sockets and sends them roiling in a dangerous hurricane-tossed moment. Then it is quiet again, and the clouds move off quickly to the west. The lush grass on the meadow remains undisturbed, the ground soft and clear of schist and granite. Two girls toss a Frisbee and a new mother walks back and forth with her baby on her shoulder. In the distance, tall buildings glisten in the dull light and the thick-trunked trees, still heavy with foliage, sway against each other, and our hectic lives are suspended for a while inside the sweet confines of the park.

A LUCKY ESCAPE

I have just discovered that stuffing and trussing a child was once a common punishment in England and Colonial New York. In 1769, Margaret Elizabeth Garnett, ten-years-old, was stuffed and trussed in front of Trinity Church with her parents' consent. So say the documents still extant in the New York City archive in lower Manhattan. I have read them all numerous times and taken careful notes and, though it is impossible to digest all the information, and necessary to accept gaps in knowledge, I believe I have found the real story.

There are many questions remaining, however. For example: why did Margaret's parents consent? And, as we are asking: why did no one watching on that day object? Apparently there was a large crowd enjoying the spectacle. Why, then, is there no record of disapproval or dissent?

I used to believe I could learn everything from books. I read voraciously. But how do I process the accusation against Margaret Elizabeth Garnett's tongue? It was too long, it stretched across the room, and her mother wanted to snip it. Why, then, wasn't her mother—clearly sadistically insane—stuffed and trussed for entertaining these outlandish thoughts? Why was the child punished instead?

The child recovered from her ordeal, but in her 20's she became a murderer. In fact, she murdered her parents and then escaped on a ship to Nova Scotia. Today, we might say: no wonder. But in the 18th century there was little compassion for parent killers.

A Conversation With A Street Vendor

Recently, I began a conversation with a street vendor. I needed socks. Did he have any bargains, I wanted to know. Yes, he said, three for five dollars. Then he handed me the socks.

"How did you know my size?" I asked.

"I'm intuitive that way," he said.

I had now been standing in front of his stall for at least three minutes. But I still hadn't looked at him. I was looking at the socks and feeling their weight. They were the wrong color and they were too thin, but I decided to buy them anyway. The reason was this: I looked up and saw the man's face. Though his eyes were out of alignment, he was handsome. He had high cheekbones, sensuous lips and almond skin. His hair was flecked with gray and he was tall. It was hard to figure out his age or why he moved so tentatively as he handed me the socks. His hand was trembling.

"Are you in pain?" I asked

"Isn't everyone?" he asked.

And then I had an intuition: this man was a vet, but which war? Did it even matter? And if I asked him more specifics—having assumed he was a vet—was I prepared for an answer?

Another customer had arrived. She was trying on a hat and chatting amiably. It sounded as though they knew each other, albeit only as customer and street vendor. Still, she was much friendlier than I was.

"What a winter," we all agreed.

"I've been stuck in my apartment without heat for weeks," the vendor said. "Can you tell I'm an amputee? I can't be slipping and sliding on the sidewalks."

I didn't want to know how he lost his leg. How could that be a life-affirming story? So I paid for the socks and left.

A STORY ABOUT A SUMMER
MORNING IN THE CITY

Recently, I saw a man walking his dog in Central Park. It was early on a summer morning and rain fresh water was swirling off puddles in the wind, the tail of a thunderstorm. There were gulls—we get a lot of them in the city, it's an island—and ducks on the pond which we call "turtle pond." Miraculously, there are many small turtles in the pond and as I stand there watching them, I sometimes imagine a giant turtle surfacing, mother of them all. I've seen children release their captive turtles into the pond. I am sure this is illegal, but it's touching; they want them to be free.

On this morning which I am talking about, the man with his dog—a large black dog—was walking near the pond and the dog kept pulling the man closer and closer to the water. The sun was fully up and the sky had turned violet and grey. The gulls cawed and the dog barked. An elderly Indian couple—he in a turban, she with legs so bowed I thought she might collapse—walked gently by, and the man said good morning to me, rolling his r, and then he smiled. By then, the big black dog had a turtle in his mouth and there was a kafuffle as we all realized we were about to witness an execution. Frantic waving and shouting at the dog's owner continued for hours, it seemed, though it was only seconds or minutes, and none of it did any good at all. The turtle was gone.

WHAT ARE WE DOING?
WHERE HAVE WE GONE?

A lynx appeared in the garden below the Belvedere. It was Shakespeare's cat, a time traveler, camouflaged by ferns, tawny green with an elongated black bindi on its forehead. I stopped walking. Was the lynx domesticated or wild? Would it allow me to stroke its head? I said, "I will be kind to you."

I ran my finger along the meridian of its Brahmin bindi. It did not stir, but its silky fur shifted under my skin. Then it scurried away. Though the park was peopled, no one else had noticed; I was alone.

I stood for a moment. There was a breeze and then a wind. I fell forward into the newly planted petunias, vividly purple, the bard's favorite. I was bereft. The cat had disappeared, not stealthily as in life, but suddenly as in myth. One minute here, the next gone.

Later, when I told the story of the lynx in the amphitheater to the assembled throng, someone asked who I was. "I am an angel," I said. "The cat is me. It stands before you. It crouches among the flowers Shakespeare planted in his garden four hundred years ago."

WOMAN WITH BAGS

She wasn't carrying a bag, she was traveling light, she said, an old habit learned from her brothers. She was wearing an elegant large-brimmed hat and white gloves. We were waiting for a bus. We started talking. "I'm on my way to a fund-raiser," she said.

"I always have too many bags," I said.

I had three that day and they were weighing me down.

"A woman's plight," she said. "We are mules."

The bus arrived and we took two seats next to one another, like old friends. A middle-aged man in a suit and a goatee and a bald head on top of a short body without any arms sat in a trance opposite us. Rubber hands poked out of his jacket, motionless. The woman turned to me and said, "I think he is praying. Let us pray for him." And she closed her eyes, put her gloved hands together on her lap, and prayed.

She got off at Lincoln Center but I was headed to the theater. I didn't want to look at the man without arms for another minute, so I fussed with my bags pretending to ready myself for departure, and then I moved to the back of the bus.

As for the rest of the evening, it was pleasant enough. The play was a good one, British actors, all well trained.

BREAST AUGMENTATION

I was traveling on the subway reading a murder mystery and sipping on a bottle of water when I looked up at the advertisements and saw a woman's breasts exposed nearly down to the nipples. My own breasts were well covered because it was cold in the train and I don't particularly like to be cold even on very hot days, and also the men on the train often stare at my breasts which are very large. I am a small woman and my very large breasts make me top heavy, and I have often thought of reducing them, the opposite of augmentation, of course. This advertisement was for augmentation and the woman's breasts and my breasts were very similar. We might have been sisters in the flesh, so to speak. Then I noticed that two men on my side of the subway car were also looking at the advertisement and one of them had an erection. I wondered if he was going to do anything with that erection, so to speak, and I looked away, but then I couldn't stop looking. But he didn't notice because he was looking at those augmented breasts and sighing deeply. I wondered if I should pull the emergency cord or not, but I was the only one who noticed the erection, apparently, and I was glued to my seat and couldn't even get up to move away, and the man suddenly noticed me, and then he got embarrassed, and he got up and moved away. He was a nice looking man but not my type really and too old for me and anyway I am married. Finally the subway ride was over and I got off and had a shower when I got home to cool off.

"I just came up to see what's going on," he said.

"Just renovating," the realtor said quickly.

No way would the realtor want his clients to know there was a problem neighbor. The kid was standing at the top of the stairs, he didn't come all the way up, and though he sounded dopey, he was polite. "On something," my husband whispered. And then we got hustled into the elevator and continued our conversation about the apartment in front of the building.

Two weeks later we were in the apartment unpacking boxes when we heard a loud thumping noise, the bass on a stereo, and because it was still daylight we tried not to pay too much attention, but that's impossible, isn't it, especially if it's a disturbing sound, or music you don't like, or a sound that may be music to some, but noise to everyone else. It went on and on and I said to my husband, "We are going to have to take care of this."

Days went by and nothing. Some noise of a television, but it was hard to tell where that was coming from and then at 3 a.m. one morning, the music again, and I am up like a shot, sleep disturbed, dream interrupted. I got dressed and wrote a note. *Dear Neighbor*, all friendly, walked downstairs, and left it under the kid's door. A dog barked. That was weird; we're in a no-pet building. Two days later I saw the kid in front of the building with a dog and introduced myself properly. "Is this your dog?" I asked. "It's my uncle's. I am in my uncle's apartment," he said.

"We've got leverage," I told my husband. "He's got a dog and he's probably in the apartment illegally. Sweet kid, though."

A few weeks, nothing, and then it started again, 5:30 a.m. this time. I got dressed, wrote a note, and went downstairs. The dog barked and the kid opened the door. "Really, no kidding, it's too loud?" he said. "Really," I said. "You are a sweet kid, I won't bother you again, but get a headset or something, okay?"

He agreed to try that and then he asked if I'd gotten my hands dirty putting the note under the door. He said he kept his place really clean. He said that right before I knocked on the door he'd been cleaning and brushing his teeth.

VALENCIA

I tried to explain to the tourists on the 1 train that I had never
been to Valencia though I could pronounce Valen—th—ia .
They were very impressed and continued to babble to me in
Spanish. "Are you having a good time? Do you like New
York?" Si si. There were 51 of THEM in the car—one of
them held up her fingers and I counted—in the midst of rush
hour on a weekday, people like me trying to get home from
work—and to make matters worse, or more interesting, most
of THEM were women or buff gay men in black sleeveless
shirts and shaved heads talking to each other at 100 miles per
hour and laughing without regard for any of the workers,
such as myself, tired and trying to get home, who might have
appreciated a seat. Oblivious. In their own tourist world, the
subway car a party venue. Nice people, I told myself, which
is why I tried to talk to them and, if I did, I thought, maybe
a gallant Spaniard from Valen—th—ia would offer me a
seat. "Are you having a nice time? Do you like New York?"
Si, si, but no seat.

At 34th Street, Penn Station, there was more trouble. A
flock of Norte Americanos dressed in white from top to toe,
toting white furniture and white picnic baskets, some kind of
international dining event, shoved their way onto the already
crowded train. I was getting out at 28th and the door was
BLOCKED so I put my fingers in my mouth and
demonstrated the New York Hail a Taxi Whistle, but it was
lost in the din.

As The World Turns

1. The realtor unlocked the door and said, "An old woman just died, please forgive the condition of the apartment. It will be fully renovated."

The workers were already there, hammering and scraping. A closet door was ajar. Coats and boots, slippers, a penny, a ribbon, a frayed dog collar with an ASPCA license, no leash I could see. I was taking inventory of a stranger's life. And in the capacious step-down living room, there was a photograph of a young girl in a prom dress and another of a handsome man in a white tuxedo jacket and bow tie. If these had been the woman's children, where were they now? Why hadn't these photographs been collected?

"All of this will end up in the dumpster," I said.

My husband pressed my hand to silence me. He wanted the apartment and so did I. It was the best we had seen.

2. Piles of unused packing tape, a broken cardboard box, newsprint, bubble wrap, dust everywhere in clumps. Sweeping creates a bridge from one life to the next, each seared floorboard canonized and cleansed, an exercise in undocumented renewal. I document it here.

3. Time is a meal consumed with appetite: at dinner parties, in each other's arms, early in the morning or late at night, as the world turns.

My Dreams Come True

It was raining this morning and the men weren't working on the retaining wall. The five-story scaffolding has been up for a while, ever since the slide last summer, but it has taken nearly a year to begin work. This is not unusual in our complex and over-burdened city, layer upon layer of infrastructure decayed or decaying since the Dutch arrived in the 17th century.

Though the noise of the hand hammering and jack hammering signals, at last, that the work has begun, it is also disturbing. Our street is a canyon and the sound ricochets. It is disconcerting to be sitting at my desk, at one end of the apartment, or go into the kitchen at the other end, and hear the sounds of the workers clearly. When the hammering stops and they are filling in cracks with a special hard bore concrete, I can even hear their conversations. "This job is my dream come true," one says. "I agree," says another.

And then they'll talk about their wives and girlfriends, and what they did to their wives and girlfriends over the weekend, or with their wives and girlfriends over the weekend. I wonder why there are no women on the job. I wonder if any of the men are gay and pretending not to be gay. I wonder if any of the workers are afraid of heights. I wonder what they'll eat for lunch.

LETTER TO THE MAYOR

Dear Mr. Mayor,

I have been meaning to write to you since you took office last January to congratulate you, of course, but also to illuminate for you various neglects perpetrated by the previous administration, neglects of which you may not be aware. I say this with all due respect as it would be impossible for any office holder in our beleaguered city to be aware of all the issues extant from previous administrations.

I know you are very busy, as are we all, Mr. Mayor, so will keep this missive short.

It's about the price of water bottles, a very egregious topic, in my view. Let me explain:

As in all other matters limning our divided city, the price of water bottles stands out, in my estimation. No underground traveler can, in their right mind, exist without a water bottle during the summer months on the subway platforms. Quite simply, it would be dangerous, for which the city might or might not have liability

Now, there are many who have purchased eco-friendly water bottles and have the foresight to fill them at home with filtered water and carry them in their bags or back packs. If we were to do a study of such water bottles, I think we would be surprised to discover the demographics of said water bottles—young. But, of course, I cannot be certain. As I am unemployed at the moment I would be happy to volunteer for this necessary survey and/or receive a small stipend (perhaps a metro card each week?).

To continue on the subject of water itself, and the bottles which contain said water. In some of the stations, there are kiosks manned by our immigrant friends from

South Asia, who sell cold water bottles packed in barrels of ice. These bottles cost an outlandish $2 whereas if we had the foresight to buy a said water bottle before entering the subway, we are usually charged $1. So my question to you, Mr. Mayor, is this: Is there any way to regulate the price of water bottles under the ground? Might the city provide giveaway bottles with your Mayoral logo visible?

But there is one more egregious instance I wish to report to you here and that is of our immigrant friends from Turkey, mostly with no English at all, selling various and sundry above ground including said water bottles, usually in two sizes. (I am only talking about the smaller one here.) And these bottles Mr. Mayor can rise in price to $3, the same price as water bottles in movie houses! But because our dear immigrant friends emerge from a culture of barter and bargaining, it is possible to bargain down to $1.50, shall we say. As a native, I know this. Tourists do not. Perhaps, Mr. Mayor, this information can be provided in city publications.

I appreciate your attention on this matter. Yours sincerely, to be sure.

MESOTHERAPY

I don't know how else to explain this really: it's like psychotherapy, but different. We study the body and various body types and diagnose various ailments our clients are not aware of because they exist on the subconscious level, and then we lay them on a table in a sound-proofed room, light scented candles, and place our hands on their backs or chest—this varies depending on the diagnosis. Once the preparations of the body are complete, we chant and pray. We pray our clients will be healed, that our tender care in the sound-proofed room will be healing. We call our clients guests, men and women of all ages, but mostly women, we're not sure why. Our guests seem very satisfied with the mesotherapy and they often make an appointment for the following week as they pay and leave. I have not mentioned payment. Of course we do charge for our services, how else to pay the rent? $50 for a face only treatment, $100 for full body. Our rates are reasonable and competitive, I am sure you will agree. Thank you for your inquiry.

CITY ENSEMBLE

Always there is something I want to say about kinship, but when I went roaming through the city alone that hot summer, I wondered where my friends were, even though I'd emailed all of them and texted a few and had a response or two. Why we are so afflicted with self-pity? Or why am I? My dears, it is tasteless.

So let me begin again: At daybreak, the pavements of the city are dark until the workers scurry to the train stations and bus stops and the Con-Ed guys—and occasionally a girl these days—set up their orange warning cones and lift the manhole covers and search for skewered wires and broken piping underneath the skin of the streets, heavy with infrastructure and history. And, one day, there are spectators—an audience—leaning into a police barrier around one of these holes and there is an abundance of concern as a man surfaces from the hole with wires around his neck gasping for air, and we all move forward to assist him. We are as eloquent in this action as we were on the day The Towers fell. No one was okay that day, but today this man will be okay, the ambulance has arrived. It is only when this small crisis is over that I hear the trombone and see the musicians on the steps of the church blowing their horns, beating their drums, pausing, playing again. We—the city dwellers—could not ask for a more inventive consolation than their melodic song.

CITY NIGHT

A friend called to remind me to leave the apartment and look up at the unobstructed sky. The moon was full that night, though it was cloudy and hard to see in its fullness, even from the Sheep Meadow in Central Park. Then it appeared, bulbous and glowing, surrounded by constellations, the sun's courtiers.

The stillness of the meadow was almost unbearable, everyone looking up at the moon. I could not stay any longer so glorious was this vision.

I left the park and meandered back towards my dank apartment. I heard crickets humming, chirping and conversing in their cricket language. A couple, standing by an open window, were arguing about a disappointing vacation. Fortunately, the crickets were louder and more insistent, and the moon, illuminated by the invisible sun, obliterated all shadows on the nearly deserted street.

CITY HAWKS

Take me along the river to see the nesting hawks, they who sit on the nest taking turns. May their patience remind us to stand silently and be kind to one another.

Notice the three chicks, you who rush to and from work each day and never stop.

Notice these hawks in the midst of our city lives; glorious birds watching over us.

Inter-Alia

HER SUITCASE WAS BLOOMING

A young woman was carrying a small gray suitcase with pink flowers etched into it. She was wearing a brown cloche hat, a brown jacket without buttons (I could see the torn threads) , a brown skirt, brown stockings and sturdy brown shoes with a small square heel. I admired her simplicity and certainty as she walked across the square past the cafe where I was having tea and cookies. I called out to her: Please join me. But she did not hear me, or perhaps she chose to ignore me, or perhaps she did not speak my language. She walked on, not a jaunty stride exactly, but purposeful. The sun caught the etched blossoms on her suitcase and brought them to life inside me.

THE STREAM'S LESSON

Today I saw a woman standing in the streambed, water to her shins. It is January and there are ice floes. I decided it was a dangerous situation so I took off my sturdy walking shoes and wool socks and waded in. I called to her, oh Madam, oh Madam, because she was an older woman, older than I am certainly. But she did not hear me, or preferred not to hear me.

I stood beside her—to her left, to be exact—and looked down into the rushing water. The tips of my toes, once manicured and tended, were now embedded in polished pebbles. I was unable to move, paralyzed. Finally, I raised one foot, then another, and I said to the woman: The weather is changing, the clouds are shifting. Suddenly there were razor sparks of light, and then a rainbow. It's a sign, I said.

If this woman was an imbecile, I was no more intelligent. Obviously, she did not want to be rescued.

Is She Blind?

Ava and Elena are watching the Spanish soaps when I arrive at the Laundromat. I ask for change, load my laundry, and hear them sighing behind me. Because I don't understand Spanish I have no idea what they are so upset about, but they seem very upset. So what is going on, Elena? I ask. The man, no good, she says.

And that is the end of her sentence.

Then I notice that the woman is carrying a long white cane. Is she blind? I ask. And I gesture blind, hands over the eyes.

Si si, Elena says, excited that I have understood, though I really haven't.

Sometimes I suggest that Elena and Ava watch an American soap to improve their English, but they have been in Nueva York for twenty-odd years and why am I trying to change them? Their lives were okay from my point of view until I met Elena on the street one day and she told me—in fractured, pidgin English—that she was looking for a new apartment –three bedroom (holding up three fingers)—four sons, (holding up four fingers), two high school dropouts, two working—one husband (holding up one finger) who comes to the Laundromat occasionally to help Elena load and fold. He speaks even less English than Elena, if that is possible, and works as a janitor at a bar downtown. How I figured this out I have no idea. I just kept asking questions. And, of course, my conclusions might be completely wrong.

A STORY ABOUT AN UNDULATING ROAD

She was walking down an undulating road. Once, only once, she turned around. She saw a small, brown-skinned child wearing an orange shirt. The shirt was very bright and fit the child perfectly. Behind the child was a tall, thin figure, and then another, and another, all equally spaced along the road. They felt like shadows of her former self, or her ancestors. Yes, perhaps they were her ancestors. In that case, the child was their descendant.

Ahead, the road was empty, shimmering in the bright summer light, not beckoning exactly, but open, like a ribbon unravelling into eternity.

Was it a procession, a pilgrimage, or a death march? They passed a farm, or what looked like a farm from her vantage on the road. It was to the right, surrounded by an electrified fence. There were signs: "Beware." She kept her distance and stopped. Strange animals romped around, playfully. Some looked like dinosaurs, others like overgrown hairy goats. They were having fun, it seemed, laughing, oblivious to the world outside the fence, or their own eccentricity.

A STORY ABOUT FRIENDSHIP

How does one describe friendship? She is a good friend, we say, but what does that mean? She wasn't a good friend is easier. She didn't show up as promised, for example. Or she was a friend just for the season, or a reason. Of course, we don't realize that at the time, do we? When we begin a friendship, and then solidify it, we assume it will be for life because we expect to mate for life, like geese, and we expect, or at least I do, that friends are the same. But they appear and disappear. And so do I. Or, I move away. Or, it's just over and I hang on and hang on. Or I stop answering emails and phone calls. Really? That's awful, I tell myself. But I do it anyway.

So here's a story that illustrates my over-all disappointment in friendship as a human institution: A friend calls to say hello after a hiatus of several months. No reason for it; we live in the same town. Just busy, right? So how are you doing? Okay, and you? I answer with the usual platitudes without launching into anything specific. Then her voice shifts into another key. She has something to say and it's about us:

I've missed you, she says.

What? I say because I am really perplexed and don't know how to answer, so I say, I don't understand.

I've missed you. I trusted you. Where have you been? When you came to dinner to meet my son, you made promises.

I made promises?

Yes. You don't remember?

No.

I offered some tea and listened to her talk about her troubled son. I still couldn't remember any promises. I said I had to get back to work. She left and I washed the tea cups and that was that. The friendship was over.

A Story About a Snake

You still recall the Sundays on the porch of your parents' summer house and the day the snake visited and your mother chased it with a broom. Speckled linoleum covered the floor, the perfect camouflage until the snake began to move. It smelled of earth and felled trees still fresh with sap. It opened its mouth and it hissed, its black-green skin, solid and unadorned, rippled on the cool floor. Then you remember the sting of anger and betrayal as you watched your mother lower the broom onto the snake's back. It could have been saved, you shouted over the high-pitched frightened voices of your parents' guests.

And the next morning it was still there. You picked it up with a child's shovel, walked it to the back of the property, and buried it.

WHEN I WAS AN AIRPLANE

I was on the tarmac waiting for take-off packed between one hundred planes and not one flying, but twenty waiting to descend, the first ten without fuel, the others without food or water, disabled by endless travel, and I thought I was an epilated bird, too vulnerable to soar. Then, suddenly, lift-off and the clouds beneath me at 32,000 feet, the possibility of free-fall in every landing. I loved the cruising best, every flash of light from the retreating sun and darkness around the curved halo of the earth, no parachute under the seats, or life rafts, or oxygen masks, the emergency doors flung open, passengers ejected from their seats, arms thrashing, as they drifted to their destinations.

There are only two places in the United States where I get lost: Los Angeles and 601 West 26th Street in Manhattan. One morning on a recent visit to LA, I was staying in Sherman Oaks with some friends—that's in "the Valley"— and I went out for an early morning run. The sun had risen in the east, but I couldn't locate it exactly because everything was so bright. What I should have done is click the "where is my car, where am I" app on my phone, but I forgot, or didn't think of it. So I set out into what looked like an easy neighborhood to navigate—a flat, grid-like layout interrupted by long avenues leading who knows where? I stopped now and again to admire the vegetation—lush and exotic—and then I continued going this way and that, telling myself: no problem, I know where I am. And then, suddenly, I didn't know where I was and the street was empty. I was jet lagged, on New York time, and that made the confusion worse. I sat on some shallow stairs leading to a pretty stucco house—I love stucco—and sipped on my water bottle. I had my phone, I could call my friends, but I didn't want to wake them. Hmm. Are there any police cruising these streets, I wondered? Los Angeles is a city of cars, but there were no cars. Too early. Then I saw a stout woman approaching the intersection. A mirage? No, she was real. Stout, carrying packages, wobbling from side to side. She greeted me in Spanish and I attempted to do the same. Donde. Good thing I knew that word. And I told her the address. No speak English, she said, and off she went, to clean someone's house, or look after someone's children, most probably. I waited a half hour. By then my friends would be up and wonder where I was, I hoped. I should have left a note, but hadn't thought of that either. I remembered the time I'd gotten lost at 601 West 26th street, a converted warehouse, huge, a city block nearly, where I had attended an event a few years back. The hallways were endless, the turnings a labyrinth, every doorway the same, and after I came out of the restroom, I couldn't find the elevator, everyone was gone, the halls deserted. Ultimately, I went down the staircase and found my way onto the street but I had been terrified, and remembered that terror, so I finally called my friends and said, "I'm having an Alice in Wonderland experience." They came to get me and walked me back, just around the corner.

GARGOYLES

She went to the waterfront late one afternoon to study the gargoyles. They were on the parapet of The Grand Hotel owned by an Indian businessman. The gargoyles arrived when he took over the hotel, one of many renovations. Before this, the parapet was just a parapet, the town of Victoria just a touristy seaside town. She had been born and raised in Victoria, she had married there, but had never visited The Grand Hotel, or its gargoyles.

She had heard about them at a party at the college where she worked. It was the dean, a former lover, who told her about them. "The gargoyles are grotesque," he had told her. "You will love them." How did he know this? She would wake and he would be beside her and she would turn towards him and, together, they discussed the underbelly of Victoria and their lives, a bonding. Too many lace curtains, they always agreed, in this very upright touristy seaside town.

And so, one afternoon, she set out to study the gargoyles. It was a pilgrimage, she thought, to seek out the ridiculous in our humdrum lives.

The front of the hotel faced the quay where the ferries docked. There was always a high wind there no matter the weather anywhere else. There were earthquakes sometimes, too, which whipped the wind and waves into frenzy. Nonetheless, it was well known that the population of Victoria always remained calm.

Observing the facade of the hotel, she noticed that the gargoyles' mouths were open. They were sucking air, growling and snarling. Their faces were bitter and vituperative. One of the gargoyles, set into the corner of the parapet, was devouring the sky.

She opened her palm-sized sketchbook and began to draw. Each gargoyle was slightly different. One had a long neck, the other a bulbous torso. She gave each of the gargoyles a name. She called the one devouring the sky "on the edge."

RECORDING A DINNER PARTY CONVERSATION

I'm preparing a dinner party and cuing up the recorder on my phone so that the conversation is documented. I am quite certain that the give and take between my erudite friends will be scintillating, as it usually is. We are all professors at the university complex in Abu Dhabi and our lives are hermetic. Dinner parties provide a welcome breather from the strain of working here on two and three year contracts. At first, it all seemed like a great adventure, until the revelations. Now we don't know exactly where we are in this tainted universe of "globalization." What a word. Though no one has so far admitted the specter of uncertainty, there is great uncertainty.

It's my guess that Jalilah will be the first to broach the subject. She's the most politically astute, and because she's been a one-term policy wonk in Washington, we cleave to her assertions and evaluations. She's articulate and knowing; we all are. That's why we are here isn't it? The chosen ones, we call ourselves, in a self-deprecating way, of course.

I'll have to do something about the ambient noise as the microphone is very sensitive. No one will think it strange that my phone is on the table as we are always awaiting calls and texts from loved ones back home. The phone goes black even as it is recording so no one will know, or will they?

I hear my guests arriving. Excuse me while I put on the soup.

HIS HEAD IS AN ORANGE

His head is an orange. His glasses are yellow. His eyes are pink. His teeth are pits running across his cheeks like fire. When he smiles, which he does often, sweet juice comes out of his nostrils. He wears a pinwheel hat that spins gently in the wind. When he lopes onto the stage, the audience gasps, and then applauds. There is no doubt that he will win the election.

A Story About a Deaf Musician

I went to the press conference to get the story. The most famous rock musician of the decade was deaf, the release said. Years ago, during a philanthropic mission to a war zone, he had witnessed the explosion of a land mine, and though he had been spared, the explosion had damaged his hearing, permanently.

The musician's handlers had kept the injury secret, and though some hearing returned in gradual increments, the musician had become tone deaf, and he could no longer decipher scales or keys. Melodies continued to effloresce inside him, but he could not release them onto the page. Nor could he play with his band any more. He had tried to mime, but this had become impossible also. He had stopped performing without explanation; now there was an explanation. In the studio, the technicians could compensate for the musician's difficulty by transposing his lyrics into sounds.

All this was explained at the press conference, and it was impressive, a good story. I listened carefully. I took notes. And then I walked home through the park. It was spring and there were many visitations: birds from Siberia, birds from Antarctica, tourists. I thought of the musician's plight, his invisible injuries. Not even his lover's words were audible to him.

HAIRY ARMS

Here I am swimming in the medium slow lane again, on my back to rest my back, and I am so close to the lane divider that I am touching the man with hairy arms in the fast lane whenever I am in the pull position with my left arm. This is really disgusting. I don't know how to avoid this unplanned touching because I have a wide stroke, my coach tells me, and I have to swim close to the edge of the lane. I want to stop and say hey, watch it, because he has a wide stroke too though he is on his stomach doing freestyle, pushing speed, doing flip turns, type A Daddy-O, and never stops to apologize or to find out if he's hurt me, though why should he? Bad luck, this guy swims at the exact same time I do. I can't wait to see him outside of the pool. In the elevator, for example. I have fantasies about this, the two of us in the elevator, alone. We get in at the same time and stand side by side. I look to my left and I don't recognize anything but his hairy arms. Do I say something? Remain quiet? Ask if he's had a good swim?

THE INTERVIEW

My source had told me a hippie was living in town. My editor wanted me to do an interview and snap a picture. What was it like to be a hippie back in the day? That was the hook, as we say.

He was homeless and, weather permitting, either slept on the beach or on a bench in the center of town, or down by the estuary. I had never seen him, and couldn't find him, at first, so I stopped a policeman I knew and asked where I could find this hippie. "Do you know where he is on any given day?" I thought that was a good question.

"Usually," the policeman said. "People complain even though he is quiet and doesn't bother anyone. I keep an eye. Give him some food now and again. In the winter he'll have to go into a shelter."

"I wonder how he ended up here?" I asked.

"Beats me," said the policeman.

This is an upscale town which has slowly been taken over by the 0.0.1%. I am not one of them and I don't even live here. I'm just a cub reporter trying to build a portfolio before I move on, hopefully into the big city. So I am always looking for interesting stories. There aren't many round here.

It was a mellow summer day and the hippie was down by the estuary splayed out on a bench. I smelled him before I saw him and though his clothes looked clean enough, they were patched together. The water was in high tide, the gulls were screeching, and there was a lot of traffic coming over the bridge, not a congenial location for an interview. I stood in front of the hippie and asked if he'd like a cup of coffee and something to eat. He said, "Sure," and we walked side by side over to Starbucks.

He was very tall with long braided hair and a whitening beard. His skin was leathery and he was wearing a vest. His chest was bare and hairy. He had colorful ornaments in his hair and around his neck. They were beautiful, obviously handmade, which he confirmed when I asked him as soon as we sat down with our drinks. He had ordered an herb tea and a scone but I had a strong coffee. I needed the coffee. Something about this man was unsettling, but what? He seemed sane, peaceful. What was wrong with him that he could live so freely and so apart? What was wrong with me that I was so disinterested.

"Have your coffee," the hippie said.

It was only then that I asked his name. It was Ed.

FIVE STRANGE THOUGHTS
NOT NECESSARILY RELATED

Note: The reader is free to change the order of these strange thoughts.

1. Frail old man. You don't know how much I love you.

2. I am raw flesh, serrated, moist, insensate. You lick my wound.

3. Life is a net: it catches living things.

4. This chair forgives my body. Soft, I sleep.

5. Has it ever occurred to you how many people we know?

Fiat Lux

A STORY ABOUT TWO BROTHERS
TALKING IN A CAFÉ

Sometime in the middle of the afternoon as they were sitting in the cafe discussing politics, the two brothers heard thunder. Or they thought it was thunder. In retrospect, they understood that the rumbling sound was not thunder, it was the tanks massing outside the city. They continued talking, oblivious to the warning sounds. The strudel arrived, and then the coffee. One of the brothers—the younger—had ordered apple strudel, the other poppy seed. They always shared their strudels.

WEATHER REPORT

A man I know went for a walk on a country lane where he had just bought himself a weekend cottage. He had checked the weather report before setting out even though it was usually wrong. The cottage—albeit substantial and winterized—was in the mountains, which has its own climate, a micro-climate; the weather is fickle there. But the man was an optimist and assumed an end of winter sun, ample in its warmth, and a benign breeze. The grasses alongside the road were beginning to regenerate and the mountains in the distance settled in a jagged configuration on the horizon line.

The man was a frugal, disciplined person, a financier in his city life, and he didn't like to dress more than once a day. If he had an appointment in the evening, he dressed for that appointment: creased trousers, a crisply ironed cotton shirt, leather shoes, and though he wasn't prepared for a country walk, he set out anyway and, once on his way, the weather report was confirmed. *It's accurate for once,* he thought. But what is beautiful from afar, or virtually through the lens of his cell phone, often becomes disfigured at close range. He hadn't noticed the clouds or taken them into consideration.

Suddenly it was raining, a driving rain, and the wind had come up so strong he had to stop and hang on to the stump of tree. There were no houses in sight and no shelter; he was completely exposed to the elements. Within minutes, his jacket, clothes and shoes were drenched, and he was afraid. *I have been hit by a tidal wave*, he thought. No cars passed and there was no cell phone coverage. He waited for the flash storm to subside before turning back to the house. By then it was dark and he had missed his appointment.

STAND FAST IN RUSHING WATER

One day in late summer, after a fierce storm, a man went fishing in the creek. The sky was still dark and the water was rushing past him, swirling into itself, devouring the bedrock, and throwing pebbles and debris onto the bank. But the man thought it was the right time to go fishing. He cast out his line and stood quietly on the bank of the rushing river. There was a sign tacked to a pylon of the bridge upriver, but it was too far away for him to see. TUBERS KEEP TO THE RIGHT. It was well known by the locals that there were dangers on this stretch of the river that worsened after a storm: jagged stones, eddies and sinkholes. The man was a local but this particular stretch of the river was not familiar to him, though he imagined he had been there before.

The fisherman walked north along the bank towards the bridge pulling his line behind him. It snagged on rocks, he lost his bait continually, but he persevered. He felt a bit chilled and began to fantasize sitting in front of a fire with a thick book. He missed his wife.

In the past, he had enjoyed the solitude of fishing, the thought of his family safely at home in a house he had built, expanded, and repaired lovingly over the years. But something had changed: The loss of his wife, his children and grandchildren all far away. Suddenly the solitude became something else: loneliness.

The man was so distracted by these troubling thoughts that he hadn't noticed the reel separating from his rod. It came undone and whipped backward, hitting him in the middle of his forehead. He fell to the ground, stunned. The rod and reel were gone, catapulting towards the waterfall a mile away. Only the red and white sinker remained, bobbing in the water by his left foot.

THE HMS LUSITANIA

I dreamt I was the captain of the Lusitania. It was 1915 and we were nearing the Irish coast when a U-boat surfaced just twenty-five yards to starboard. These facts are all wrong, of course, but that was my dream. And it continued: I saved the Lusitania. It did not sink. No one died.

This is a either a story about changing history or not accepting fate, or both. I refused to accept the great liner's fate. I stayed on the bridge when the torpedo hit—I was the Captain after all—and after a successful evacuation of all the passengers, I roamed the empty, smoldering deck. I admired the beauty of the portholes, the creak of the timber, the soft swell of the sea, and the salty lubricious spray where all life began.

After the bombardment, against all expectation, the ship remained seaworthy and level. Nonetheless, the evacuation was necessary. For the most part, it was orderly, but a few passengers were panic-struck and jumped to their certain deaths. So I am revising history again: not everyone survived. As for me, I was the last soul on board what turned out to be—ultimately, in another lifetime—a sinking ship. I remained steadfast and serene. I watched the sunset and, the next morning, I watched the sunrise.

Throughout most of this ordeal, the offending U-boat remained at the bow of the ship. Then in the morning, like most nocturnal creatures, it departed silently. By evening of the second day after the attack, rescue ships arrived, and all but a few passengers returned safely to port, but I stayed aboard. Using the constellations and my intuition, I steered the wounded, limping ship to ground.

In Transit

The railroad station was a hut in the middle of a forest, a way-station, as capacious as a barn, unheated, soiled. The floor was compressed sand, sifted and layered, like the silt at the bottom of the river, moist and dense with cadavers and ash.

A man and a woman sat on a bench and waited for the train. They had been walking for days, eating berries and ferns. The ferns were bitter and caught in their throat. The man spit. The woman choked and heaved. They had sent their children ahead with strangers more than a month ago.

They were hungry and embarrassed by their hunger. The woman wanted an apple. She had been dreaming of an apple. The man wanted bread and had been dreaming of bread. He was chewing on his tongue.

Her hair was blonde, her face wide. A friendly and open face, a smile without teeth from the months they had been on the road sleeping in shacks, scrounging for food, like wolves. The man was dark-haired, his eyes cerulean blue. He had been a handsome man, loved by many women, a loving, handsome man, a husband now.

The air was fetid and still, high summer. A desert in the midst of the forest, an abandoned train station. But the man and the woman did not notice its abandonment. They sat. They waited.

In ordinary times, it should not be difficult to locate a source of sustenance, a zone of safety, ones' children, a train.

TRACK 218

I've been to the train station before but not with strangers and they are all women and I have no luggage and by accident I've brought the broken red shopping cart but it's empty. I stand in line at a series of information booths. All the men behind the windows are in uniform.

They are patient with my inquiries. Where? How? They hand me printed cards with track numbers and tablets with routes etched on touchstone screens. Where is the red cart? I could use it now. My hair parts and turns silky so I take selfie pictures and record sounds on the platform—the air, the trammel, the smoke and, in my left ear, someone whispering: Track 218. Track 218.

THE SIEGE

It begins early in the morning. First, the gathering of troops on the parade ground, then the drill, preparations for an anticipated skirmish. Is a skirmish the same as a battle? Has the battlefield shifted?

Later, they set out on forested roads. It was winter. The soldiers—all so young—were wearing snowflakes on their ears, pajamas, and thin socks. They had been torn out of bed for an exercise, a maneuver, they had been told. But they lost their way and staggered behind enemy lines into bloodied terrain where corpses of the enemy lay decaying in the road and on the side of the road. That is when the barrage started.

A soldier turned his head to admire a waterfall and weeping willows, the landscape of his youth, he said. Another started humming a tune and began to dance.

The sound of jets roused her from sleep. Outside, the still wintry overcast sky lay speckled and worn. Now there were navy blue fighter jets overhead in a re-configured flight path. They approached and then veered away, their engines thrumming and spewing fumes. She watched with incredulity as one plane spun downward nose first into the settlement of houses just yards away from her windows. Only poor people lived there and it was as though they had been targeted by the machines designated to protect them, those enormous navy blue planes with white markings and red lettering. Eerily, there was no sound or smoke as the buildings swallowed the plane's body and then its tail. All was in stasis until hysteria, and then motion, erupted. Ambulances arrived. In the distance, a woman with curly black hair was sunbathing on a sand dune, oblivious and inured. It's a scene she'd witnessed before: Sevastopol after the Liberation, that famous photograph from May, 1944, men and women in the rubble of a shattered city catching the sun, and smiling.

It was cold and dark, the dead of night, past curfew, as we approached our house. The war was nearly over, but there was still danger. Resistance fighters were tunneling through the mountains into the villages and taking them over. So we were fearful and remained vigilant.

Sometimes, however, life went on as if it were normal, or perhaps we had become accustomed to pretending that it was normal. That night, we had gone to visit friends and Joaquim had challenged Peter to a game of chess. I stayed in the kitchen talking to Louise, as women do. We were both grateful we didn't have children to protect during the horrible, long war, but wanted to start a family soon. Suddenly it was late and we had a discussion about whether we should stay or leave. I don't know why we made a reckless decision. I could sense trouble; my intuition was never wrong. And when we arrived at the house, we saw a light. Unwanted guests—the fighters—were helping themselves to our supplies.

We scurried down the path like ferrets. We were animals now, so the analogy came easily. In and out of hedge grows, head down, arms swinging wildly, running and running until the sun came up. Occasionally we stopped and turned over rocks to search for worms, a source of protein, and also fennel. Fennel, with its biting licorice flavor, had become our favorite food.

The soldier who captured us was from my village. We had gone to school together. He was wearing a navy blue coat, army issue, and a powder blue woolen cap that matched his eyes. His face had aged, the once smooth skin was now rutted with experience. Cigarettes had roughened his voice. He was no longer insouciant, he was grave. He reminded me of an actor I had once admired.

I stepped forward and reached out for him. Perhaps if we could touch, I thought. But his pistol was pointed at Joaquim's heart and then it was pointed at my heart.

We began our silent ascent into the mountains. The trail was narrow. Tall grass spires swished over us with a rush of air. A small deer crossed our path and began grazing a berry patch. Soon it was night again. The soldier's flashlight illuminated the path, and then the cave. Was that a smile? I wasn't certain.

The cave was a safe haven where we could rest and talk, the soldier said. After that, our fate was not in his hands.

THE CAVE

They lived in a cave in the mountains. It was well furnished. The ground was mined, but this was of no consequence as they had purchased special shoes. These shoes detected mines within a six foot circumference. One foot slowly in front of the other foot. Progress was slow, but this also was of no consequence. Because they had no place to go, each day had become predictable.

In the morning they searched for food and water, berries and leaves. Their digestion had reverted to this vegetarian diet. They followed the bears' spoor which guaranteed a meal by midday. Their stomachs rumbled as they remained focused on their task. They had no words to explain their feral existence.

There were other caves in proximity, all well-furnished. Clusters of men, women and children. They might once have been relations or neighbors, but this, also, was of no consequence. As an observer, one would say they were people of disparate and unknown association. They had re-formed themselves. They had no history.

TO FLEE (A VERB)

Taking some things I want. Leaving some things I'll never want. Taking some things I think I'll want. Leaving some things I thought I'd want. Taking some things I'll never need. Taking some things I'll always need. Taking some things to store. Leaving some things forevermore.

THE ANT FARM

She was reading about ants in a novel. Why were the ants there? She stepped inside the protagonist's head and tried to figure it out. Oh frabjous day! Within minutes she saw what the characters saw and felt what they felt: revulsion. Though miniscule, the ants were grotesque. A lab technician—one of the characters in the story—removed glass from one of the tanks and explained that ants never tried to escape. They existed to service the regal few: a Queen, her Consort, the Courtiers. This biological arrangement was aesthetically pleasing to scientists, apparently. Then, a few paragraphs later, the ants worked frenetically to dismember a captured scorpion. She stopped reading; this was too much. But the next morning on the way to work, she began reading again. Why did she find the story so compelling? The diorama of the ant farm—two dimensional on the page—had become three dimensional in her head: the ants, their society, the scorpion, the lab technician. Pure evil in an unquestioning world.

MY MOTHER IS AN OLD TREE

My mother is an old tree. My mother is a felled tree behind the house. My mother burns. My mother did not always love her life or us. My mother carried her murdered mother onto the porch. My mother killed the soldier with a spoon.

A Story About a Farmer in Wartime

A farmer was standing on his porch at sunrise. Slicers rained down from the sky and erupted in his fields. Several landed close to the house, sparked, and ignited the dry grass. The fire smoldered and shifted direction, sparing the house.

The farmer thought, "I have to feed my family. I have to plow in some seeds. It will be summer soon." It was as if he didn't see the fire that was surrounding the house. Perhaps he was in a daydream that carried him somewhere else, his idyllic childhood, or his vacation in Sicily when he had turned twenty. Now he was forty—too old to be conscripted, too young to succumb to despair.

A whooshing sound in the distance brought him out of his daydream, the grasslands in the distance burned and the man remained on the porch and thought. He heard his wife and children screaming, and then they were silent, and he knew they were gone.

He walked into the barn and pulled out a burlap bag of alfalfa seed. He walked into a field and tossed the seeds into the still unfertilized furrows.

He remembered his parents and how they had encouraged him. "You have a good head on your shoulders," his father had always said. His teachers agreed. But they were all dead now—his parents, his teachers—living only in his memory. It was strange how he could always conjure them in the field as he was tossing seed. Why had they not prepared him for this war?

He was decapitated in an instant. His head fell into the furrow, the marigold eyes startled open. The headless torso sank to its knees, remaining upright like a groundhog feeding on a nut, or a congregant at prayer.

Within days the seeds had sprouted in the furrows. But no one was there to harvest them.

THE OUTCASTS

Once upon a time a man, an outcast, lived inside the crater of an inactive volcano. His skin was scarred by whippings. He had such outlandish thoughts that even his parents did not want to hear them when he was a boy. It was they who had sent him to live inside the volcano, exiled like Cicero had been exiled from Rome. In fact, Cicero was also living inside the volcano and the two men were companions of sorts; they helped each other survive hardships, sharing food and scrap timber for fires and shelter.

Underneath the volcano's footprint was a lake of ice though this was not known to the two outcasts for a long time. The volcano was only temporarily inactive, it was coming to life again, and the ice was melting. But one starry night the gurgling sound of the water alerted them and they began their trek across the valley, out of exile, and down into the valley where life had continued happily without them. The lava was slippery and the men lost their grip from time to time, but they leaned into the mountain and kept going, conversing at length and shouting encouragement to each other. Soon they were in a village which, to their surprise, was empty of human habitation.

The room is cluttered when she arrives, and there is a vinegary smell. A natural cure for cockroaches, she heard someone say. Pour vinegar into the cracks, let it evaporate at its own speed. Is she evaporating? She takes off her Gortex jacket, folds it neatly, and places it mindfully on the bed. Grey army issue wool blanket. She's noting all the details. Her mind is occupied. *How long will I stay? Where are my books? Where are my clothes?* If only she could ask these questions. If only someone could answer them. But the door is shut, she is alone, and the corridor is silent. The room is illuminated by one light bulb hanging on a wire. *I am empty handed. I have no belongings.* This is where her thoughts stop. She sits on the bed next to her jacket. *The past is baggage enough, if only I could make use of it.* She walks to the window and contemplates the vista. Mountains in the distance, fields touching the brick wall, shacks and barns. All in the present tense. Dogs, horses, ploughs, a well in the centre of the village.

AFTER THE SLAUGHTER

inspired by Caspar Friedrich

After the battle, he ran into the woods. Now he was watching the soldiers from behind the bushes, three men dressed in capes and hats, their masks discarded and lying on the fallow ground, out of time or, perhaps, of this time. They were conversing intently, though he was too far away to hear their words clearly. Two of the men had bloodied brows, the other a bloodied hand. The landscape, once so marvelous and true, was tainted, the hill falling away under the soles of their muddied shoes. The sky darkened, a gibbous moon, a star, the funnel of the universe collapsing and then expanding above them. He moved closer and heard them say—clearly suddenly—that they would return to kill, the battle was half won and only half over; they would destroy the village, slaughter all that remained alive. He thought of his family— all gone—his friends—all gone—and the layby on the side of the road where he had first made love.

Yet another eyeless day in Gaza, yet another marriage in an orchard on a hill, yet another sandstorm predicted and, in the final stanza, promises of redemption and ripened plums. In the distance, unknown fallen soldiers wrapped in linen reiterate prophecies. Closer still, jails over-run with vermin and lice, abandoned moonlit vistas, the crevice widening as an invalid nation retreats lamely to its rest. And, finally, Angels float on the surface of the Red Sea as herons stalk ancient mosaics. They walk alone.

We retreated to the dead side of the planet as we had been instructed. It was a celluloid environment encased in lead. There was no escape.

We began to run but the air was so thin we choked. Child beggars were crawling along the edges of this world and the next. We boarded a monorail. Brahmins with oversized suitcases told us they were escaping into the hills. The monorail rocked, the earth heaved. There was no outside, only inside. Inch by inch year by year within our lifetime we had moved closer to the sun. Warnings abounded, all unheeded.

My lover was soft and there was no heft to his flesh, no gravitas, and I was eroded, broken. I held my lover's hand and pulled him along but even this tenderness could not save us.

Finally, we arrived at the artificial garden but Adam and Eve had fled.

FIVE THOUSAND YEARS

for Liat

Bombs are falling in Gaza, rockets are flying near Haifa. Birds that were twittering are now silent, or dead. They no longer greet the morning.

A man on the corner is begging for food. An unhappy woman is working in a bank. Children are playing games in the rubble.

No one thinks, why are we here? What is our purpose on earth? Why are we destroying ourselves and each other?

Five Thousand Years and all wisdom has fled. To love or fight? To cherish life or end it?

CHILDREN TO LOVE

*for the children of Gaza, Israel,
Iraq, Syria, Congo & Afghanistan*

These children I love, because they are children, I love them. That girl, that boy, a safe haven somewhere. All the trees had been felled, the earth was barren behind the house, but the children played, and their games continued, and belonged to them.

I had brought them all a gift and handed it to the girl. She unwrapped it slowly, its paper and ribbon dangling onto the floor, nearly tripping her as she walked away from me towards her friends and said, "Thank you for this gift." She spoke clearly in a universal language though she was very small. How old was she? Three? Four? I can hardly remember now.

We had escaped the bombing, a temporary reprieve. Rockets and mortars stored in underground tunnels and caves surfaced sporadically, yet the children continued playing, and whenever the adults gathered, it was an occasion. There was music, a bit of dancing, food. We told stories, we made love, we slept.

And we loved the children and gave them small gifts. We owned nothing. We possessed nothing. Only the children mattered.

She is wearing leather sandals and a black dress that grazes her ankles. Her blouse is pulled tight in a crisscross around her bosom. Most notable, there is a large coin hanging around her neck on a tong. Her deceased husband bought her this talisman in a market in South Sudan.

"How can money be purchased?" the reporter asks.

She takes out a box of cigarettes, lights one, and inhales deeply.

"I am surprised you smoke," the reporter says.

"I have been out of the country for twenty years," she says. "I've never seen The Sopranos. My clothes are out of fashion."

She gets up to leave, hugging a folder to her chest. Fully extended, it is now evident she is small in stature, diminished by the atrocities she has witnessed in the camps.

THE FOREST

for all the children

Welcome to the dark forest with its mushroom lacquered stumps. Up above, a canopy of leaves dense with summer light. Below, a stream running wild over eroded rocks, a purple cloth caught on a barnacled root, pebbles saturated with color. We paint our faces red, green, and blue, the sun hissing above us, insects feeding on our flesh.

Did you know that fish squat in the water waiting for bait, that they will do this even after we are gone? Therefore, tell me: What will save our world? What will open the hearts of warriors? Rockets or trees?

Morning news report: The airport has been evacuated. I had a walkie-talkie on the seat beside me and shouted into it: "I'm in the parking lot. There are no cars. I am the only one here."

A voice answered: "I am in the cafe. I will wait for you."

I circled the parking lot several times but could not decide on the right spot. Infinite choices and I did not want to be there. The engine idled.

The sky was gray, the clouds moving swiftly across the abandoned runways. Gulls feasted on the debris of rotting in-flight dinners, their plastic wrappings torn open.

The walkie-talkie crackled. "I am still waiting for you," the voice said.

I did not answer. I drove around the empty parking lot one last time before exiting the airport.

There were no cars on the road, no planes in the sky, and the bridge I'd taken just an hour ago had shattered.

A long-married American couple were having dinner in an inn in Japan high in the mountains. It was a small inn and they were the only guests. The air was moist and clear. Words dripped easily and the man and the woman, celebrating their 20th wedding anniversary, were content.

A live fish was brought to the table, a great delicacy, they had read. The fish was speared in the middle with a wooden stick. It blinked knowingly.

The woman said, "I won't be able to eat this fish."

The man said, "We will insult the innkeeper if we do not eat this fish."

Several minutes had passed. The innkeeper came to their table to ask, in halting English, if everything was alright. The man tried to explain that though they knew the fish was a great delicacy, a gift from the innkeeper, they would not be able to eat the fish.

"We would like some rice," the woman said, miming eating rice with her chopsticks.

The innkeeper went into the kitchen to get some rice. He said to his wife, who was the cook, "These Americans will not eat the fish." Then they both laughed.

During the occupation, the inn had been closed for a while, but then it re-opened. American soldiers came to visit often and they were rude and condescending to the innkeeper and his wife. This is when they decided to change the menu to "great delicacies." The live fish was a favorite among the soldiers.

NOMADS

I'm writing these words lying on my left side on a freshly made bed. The sheets are off-white, a cream color. My tongue is resting on my teeth. The window is open and there is a fresh breeze off the water. Boats, fishermen, a child running naked on the beach, the wafting smell of spices cooking.

I'm lying quietly, drifting in and out of sleep. The journey was arduous, a lot of tumult, constant danger. Now, finally, a respite.

Have I mentioned the desert crossing? Day and night we walked the dunes bypassing the crevasses of history, or so we thought. Long-ago stars flickered as we darted through the dry landscape.

We seek shelter from the chaos, dragging once again into exile. Maybe this time we'll stay awhile, we'll rest awhile.

I thought I'd write a story about the new puppy in our family who has amber eyes with green trim, a delicate head with droopy ears and chocolate fur. That would have been story enough as she is completely adorable and we are all in love with her. But then there was a knock on the door, the farmer across the road delivering logs for our wood stove. We stepped outside onto the pine needle carpet dusted with snow and there it was: a pileated woodpecker more than a foot long. All the ornithologists had thought it was extinct. They were wrong. I take a moment to think about this. I sip my tea. I ignore the newspaper with its dire warnings and when I do open it I try to pay attention to the good news buried somewhere on page 10, but the print is so small, it barely exists, so I decide to write my own headlines: OUR NEW PUPPY ARRIVES. THE PILEATED WOODPECKER RETURNS.

IDEA FOR A KIDNAPPING RESCUE

At the beginning of the week, there was news about the smart girls kidnapped in Nigeria. There were demonstrations in many cities and many countries. Very large nations contemplated sending soldiers to find the girls, but this never happened. Why didn't it happen? The girls had been captured *en masse*, more than 200 of them.

It might help, I thought, if we all sang a song once a day in honor of these lost girls, perhaps in the morning before breakfast, or when we are showering, or combing out our hair in our *tutti frutti* rooms with full length mirrors and plants on the windowsills.

Every kidnapped girl has an empty room; she is no longer there. The room is a clean slate, all history erased, a new beginning, a fresh start, where a child can be a child again, positive and hopeful, and free of a cruel fate such as kidnapping.

Sunlight is streaming through bubbled windows. Time slips. The girls are here, as before, tucked into their beds for the night.

Musa

THE ARTIST AND HIS MUSE

Inspired by a de Kooning painting

Recently, an artist told me about a model he destroyed with his brush. She did not realize his intention so continued to pose for him, day after day, week after week. He paid her well, or well enough, he told me. And she was flattered by his interest and attention. "I understood her from the inside out and the outside in," he boasted. "I could sense her moods and posed her accordingly."

One day the model arrived on a bicycle. It had been a gift from her grown son who thought she would enjoy the exercise and freedom. She lived about two miles away from the artist and was reliant on a tram which didn't run very frequently. The artist was often angry at these unforeseen delays and was therefore pleased about the bicycle. "But she soon smashed it," the artist said. "The frame was twisted around her torso, bruising her limbs and imprisoning her spirit."

Even as she recovered, the woman came to pose for the artist, though travel was even more difficult for her. She understood that the consequences of a failed experiment were grave and she did not want to fail. The artist drew her with care, and she responded with devotion. But her body was now distorted and she walked with a limp. After several months, the artist began to loathe her. He drew her heart pulsing, her breasts pumping, and her flesh burning. Because he could no longer idealize her as a great beauty, he destroyed her. Hands, face, torso, breasts, and feet flowed like lava onto the artist's sandaled feet.

THE MUSE

She sat at her desk not knowing how to begin. She read a poem hoping the poem would stir a beginning. The poem did not stir a beginning.

Her muse had fled in the night. All that was precious and luminous had fled. All that was precious and luminous had been stolen, and she is like a blind woman, her fingers tracing the nuanced lines on the surface of a stone, as friable as plaster, as soft as sponge.

She was bereft. The muse was her lover, the lover was her muse. Now she could feel her dreams but not remember them. They too had fled, or evaporated. Where does a dream go when it cannot be remembered?

She sat at her desk and said, *I will imagine*. She imagined an embrace and then a kitchen exuding the odor of garlic and wine, a cacophony of voices, pots, and stories. The muse came to life. The muse spoke.

Scent of mint rising from the river, fish playing between the children's toes, nearly lunchtime. Wind in trees rushing into clouds, clouds efflorescing across the sky, sky pulsing into stars, stars becoming endless night, night looping back to day, earth rotating potatoes on a spit, chicken cooking with onions and herbs, inspiration of appetites.

I only see shapes, I only see color, I only see light, I scrape the landscape with my palette knife.

The Dream Reporter

I have always believed that there is an argument to be made for tracking dreams, to be a reporter of dreams. The argument is conventional, that is to say, based on convention. But at what point, I am asking, does innovation become convention? And at what point are we obligated to disregard convention and to challenge the dream reporter?

Tracking dreams is an exercise in awareness and self-discovery, we are told. But what if the dream reporter is an informant? What then?

For example, though the dream reporter does not use electronic devices, he listens attentively and appears empathic. He shakes his head. His words are kind. He professes understanding, even compassion. And he is proceeding with the task of tracking dreams with what he perceives to be our implied permission. The dreams are there to be tracked so he will track them. Then, at the moment of reporting the dream to the public, he reveals our deepest and most strange fantasies. So is he friend or foe? Innovator or protector of the status quo?

There is an artifact known as the dream catcher. This is available to the dream reporter, if he chooses to make use of it. He usually does. Let the record show that the dream catcher was devised by Native people many eons ago as a sacred object. It is built like a spider's web and woven with feathers. And now it has been commandeered by the contemporary dream reporter for a different and more sinister purpose. The purpose is not unlike a credit check. Find out what the person applying for a loan has in the bank. Find out what the dream catcher has caught of the dreamer's dreams.

It is a mistake to assume the dream reporter has a magical temperament or magical abilities. He is simply an employee of the state who has been trained at the taxpayer's expense.

DREAMS

Poets have written about the country of dreams. In this country there are familiar roads and pleasant laybys, but also vectors, elisions and chasms. The sun sets as expected, or not. At times, the earth refuses to turn, or when it turns, the meadows bloom.

The dream may signify utopia or dystopia. Naked children play, or drown. A gray-haired man in a tweed suit sits alone at a table in an expensive restaurant, his face illuminated by candlelight. A woman goes into labor and weeps, or laughs.

FOUR

A story of four paragraphs, four lines each. There were always four of them. Four sets of eyes, four voices, four seasons, four cups, four saucers, four recorded conversations, one leading to another until the conversation stopped and the story ended. There could not be a fifth because the fifth did not exist. And if it did exist, he could not find it.

And then there are images, repeated four times. Open sun roofs, windy days, oceans and, in the distance, wheat fields and barns. The world is symmetrical, two on each side, two hemispheres, two nations, two hundred million people, four hundred million all together, a planet with four moons, all shining brightly.

He is grateful that the story of four can speak, that he is able to receive it—its tender words, an open sun roof, wind tossing his hair, the smell of manure, the sound of birds, a dog barking, a tractor. The story ends. The fifth line and the fifth paragraph remain invisible. He has arrived at the end of the story of four in four paragraphs.

THE WHITE DRESS

after a painting by Thomas Wilmer Dewing

Inside a golden frame, inside a sunlit room, glowing with affection, two women are facing the sea, one in a chair, naked, head bowed, the other in a long white dress, the hem green with algae. The naked woman steps onto the horizon and then out of the frame. Then the sun shifts and there are ghostly reflections, chimères, the Haitians call them. In the distance, the ocean beats back the future while, inside the room, the rod iron chairs, set at angles in the sand, remain fixed, until the dunes collapse.

READING TO AN EMPTY ROOM

I just found out I'd be reading a poem in a famous cafe downtown. That is, I've been asked to read a poem I have not as yet written. Had I written the poem, I could prepare for the reading.

A man called to invite me to read. I was in the park gardening that day, planting bulbs and raking leaves, my Saturday occupation. The park is pure poetry, I always say. And I was in the park, in the midst of pure poetry, when my cell phone vibrated. (I turn it off but still pay attention, an oxymoron.)

I put down the rake and moved away from the other gardeners. The caller had a low voice and, at first, I thought it was my husband, that there was some emergency, but he would not have disturbed my day if there was no emergency, and the number that came up was not known to me.

Your submission, the man said without introducing himself, I like it very much. What had I sent him? Who was he? From what journal? I'd like you to read, he said. Not this poem necessarily, but one or two others. A work in progress is fine.

The sensation of the empty room began. It's dark in the room and it smells of beer and burning candles, but there is no one there. I am at the podium facing an empty room. I clap my hands. Bravo, I say, and wait patiently for more applause, accolades so silent only I can hear them.

Amore

GENERIC LETTER TO A LOVER FAR AWAY #1

Dear _____,

I am back in the city after a full summer away. In the country, I dreamt of car horns and rain. In the city I dream of birds and rain. In either place there is a magnet riveting us to the center of the earth. I wonder if you know this. Quite frankly _____, you live without awareness of the sensory delights of our environment. City or country you are oblivious. But let me not berate you. Let me continue with my discussion of country vs. city.

For example, the birds flock to their destination without reading maps or relying on GPS. They follow an unknown path—unknown to us, at least. This path is mythic, a labyrinth. Am I making sense? In the pond—remember the pond?—we swam with toads and salamanders. You were horrified and had your warts removed attributing them to the toads. So now your skin is smoother than mine.

This summer, without you, I rested on the pine needles. The needles were sharp and cut into my flesh. Did I mention I was splayed like a deer after a kill? Open, remorseful, unrequited. Did I mention I was innocent?

I remain,

Very sincerely yours,

_____

MEXICO

When I was in love, I sat in the front seat of the car. And when I fell out of love, I sat behind the driver, my head against the glass partition. The road and my memory of love drifted away.

When I was in love, and we arrived at the farm where my husband was born and raised, I played with the donkeys in the corral. And when he took the journey north and I fell out of love, I went to the farm where he was born and raised to stay with his family. I ate vanilla ice cream cones with his sister's children. Tumbleweeds whirled in a dusty wind, darkening the sky.

He is north of the border and I am in Mexico waiting for him. I have no children and I am out of love. Many years have passed, many days. The sun rises every morning and I have put out feeders for the birds and planted my garden.

THE BRIDE WORE WHITE

The bride wore white though the dress was plain satin without ruffles or decoration. A plain white dress with a straight across- the-breast bodice and a straight across-the-hips skirt with a slight bustle in the back, an echo of the distended stomach and, in its own way, a disguise.

The guests were waiting around the four poster bed. The posts were a dark oak, the bed all white, like the bride and her dress. The bed cover was plain, without flounces.

The bride entered stage left. The bride, the guests, the four poster bed, the white satin dress, the distended stomach with the quickening child kicking impatiently against the bride's diaphragm. The guests saw the kick and then heard a small voice say, "If you are searching for a bit of news, here I am."

What century are we in? Had the fetus already been to broadcast school?

Silently, the guests observed the bride. Her tresses, long and thick, framed her masked face. The mask was skin tight, sucked into the flesh of her face, every pore saturated with white-out. Only her lashes and red cupid lips surfaced in three dimension. "She doesn't want to be identified," someone murmured. It was one of the guests, an old man standing serenely against the wall, separate from the others, but also one of them.

Then the groom arrived. Descriptions of him abound, available in myths. He was a Prince Charming, a man of every woman's dreams, and so on. There is no need to repeat all these stories here. Suffice to say that the bride turned to find him standing at her back. She jumped into his arms and wrapped her legs around his torso, capturing him for all eternity. In one dramatic and chivalrous gesture, the groom ripped the mask from the bride's face as the guests sighed.

We are sitting side by side in a darkened movie theater. The previews are about to begin. If only he would touch me. It is our third date, please touch me I want to say. He'll probably want to talk about the plot, right? It's not even that he's so attractive, at least not to me. I wonder if he's feeling the same, in reverse?

I sit up a bit straighter in my seat and feel a pimple on my back rub against my blouse. What if he undresses me? Should I warn him beforehand? Shall I say, I have a pimple on my back. There is a run in my panty hose. My bladder is full?

He eats his popcorn without offering me a morsel. That was a test when he asked me if I wanted my own popcorn. I said no, but I meant yes, because I wanted to share his popcorn and eat out of the same container. I thought that might be intimate. But he hasn't offered me any. In between bites, he either puts the container on the floor, or on the empty seat next to him.

My fingers are twitching like they did when I was a child and my mother told me I was doing something wrong. I try to concentrate on the opening scenes of the movie. I put my elbow on the arm of his chair hoping he'll take my hand. But he doesn't take my hand.

WHY?

Why do I enjoy both solitude and crowds? And why is it so humid today? Why do animals and flowers please me more than people? Why do my friends beat me at Scrabble most of the time? Why does it matter? Why would anyone announce on FB that they are feeling poorly because of such and such and such and such and expect instantaneous sympathy? Why is it a relief when jury duty is over and you will never be called again because in six years you will be over 75? Why is that happy news and not grim news? Why is Chris, the lifeguard, still so huge he can hardly get onto the chair? Why did an oversized woman sit next to me on the bus and think it was insulting when I moved away? Why did she give me a dirty look, make a rude remark, and say something out loud to her friend about my rudeness? Why don't I care that a friend is mad at me and sending me anguished emails about herself and her situation? Why is a stranger on the bus talking about her love life on her cell phone so loud everyone can hear her? Why doesn't she care that we all can hear her? Why doesn't she let the guy go?

THE MAN WHO HAD A BABY

Once upon a time, a man had a baby. He called to say he was delivering the baby, it was coming out slow and easy and he wasn't in any pain. I don't know why women complain, he said, this doesn't hurt at all.

Men don't have pain when they deliver babies, I thought. Well, bravo.

When I arrived at the man's house he was standing up making phone calls to more friends and asking them to come over to see the new baby that he had delivered so painlessly. He was wearing a tall Stetson hat cocked back on his head and cowboy boots and spurs.

When he finally put down the phone he was even more energetic and cheerful. I love babies, he said. I really love babies. The birth of this baby was a breeze. I am going to have more babies.

Then I looked around for the baby, but it was nowhere to be seen. Where is the baby, I want to see the baby, I came over to see the baby, I said. How did you manage to have a baby?

New technology has made it all possible, he said. My store of choice is on Fifth Avenue just south of St. Patrick's Cathedral. The midwife was wonderful. Let me give you her card. Within an hour, you will have a baby, designed in your image—hair, eyes, skin color. The delivery, as I have said, is painless. Completely painless.

GENERIC LETTER TO A LOVER FAR AWAY #2

Dear_____,

So I am feeling a little peek-ed this morning as the Brits would say. I have seen you on FB—mutual friends—at a birthday picnic party in _____'s back yard, red and white checkered tablecloths, a band playing (it was a video no less), and to say I was not invited is an understatement; it is as though I don't exist. Whose lover are you? Everyone's always or no one's never?

Though it is summer, I note that you are dressed in wool and sitting arm in arm with a back I do not recognize, elbows and shoulders touching. Please state the obvious, *sotto voce* if you must, and confirm my observation: there are sea grasses seeding, but not in your back yard, only mine. Fecundity.

So, you are not telling again. Okay, I will recline in the hammock on our once happy porch and rest. But you should know by now that continuing silence will... what? Contain me.

Yours once again ever so sincerely, I remain,

_____

DIORAMA

One again she had a dream about the man in the Brooks Brothers shirt. He was an angel, pale and wiry, barely visible against the bright background of the field in which they stood. The scene was a living diorama, but this was an oxymoron. A diorama is not living, it is dead.

The man was leaning against a tree and the woman was standing next to him. Their bodies touched, but only ethereally. The sun was high and bright—controlled weather conditions—and the moon was visible in the eastern sky. They looked through the glass into the darkened exhibition hall.

Observers stopped to stare at them. The crowd murmured.

He was an angel, woven of gossamer thread, his shirt—purchased and therefore known—was the only emblem of the real world beyond the diorama. If she moved, the diorama would be destroyed. If she tried to lean closer, the man would fall over and melt. She would melt. All that would remain of him would be the Brooks Brothers shirt. All that would remain of her would be the memory of the shirt.

AT THE COUNTRY CLUB

It was sunny, a summer sunny day, humid. They were sitting at the shallow end of the pool at an upscale country club. Life was sweet, they always said. They had no complaints.

They were both dressed in white halter top bathing suits, wrap-around batik lounge skirts and designer sun glasses, sexy well-manicured women in their 40's. Married, two children each, all in day camp, husbands in the city working.

A waiter came by and took their order: iced green tea. "Let us add more cold to this day," one of the women said. "I am cold enough," said the other. This was a coded comment about her lover. It disturbed her friend's repose. "What do you mean?" she asked.

"I dream of him while he dreams of others," she said.

She spoke slowly, the words jammed in her throat. Her eyes were vacant behind her glasses.

Generic Letter to a Lover Far Away #3

Hello my love,

Time has passed and your voice has faded to a tattoo inside me. Slumbering one moment, alert the next, I become animated by a sentence, a word, or a breeze. Some say I am not permitted to this sensation of the tattoo or to hum your favorite tune in an effort to evoke you. Your voice: a harp inside a bell. The bell: clanging.

I might be walking along the street peacefully when I hear you, smooth as velvet. Though unexpected, you are welcome and I want you to stay.

I have heard through various vines that you are a continent away. Thus the miracle of our continuing intimate connection.

Have I mentioned that I erased all the photographs of you from my phone? This was rash and I am now doubtful of regret. Can you please send me a replacement or two forthwith.

Sincerely, I remain...

————————

THE LOOSENED WHEEL

When the car snapped open on the rutted roadway over the tide-driven river, brackish water flooded the cabin. She tried to mount the wheel as she gasped for air but it had come loose from its moorings. The sun glared and then sank into the horizon.

Hours later when the emergency vehicles arrived, they found her body clinging to the top of the car which had been carried onto the embankment. She almost made it, the workers all said. She was strong, persevering, but had lost her traction.

CERTAINTY WAS HER MANTRA

Once upon a time she knew exactly what to do and how to do it, what to say and how to say it. Certainty was her mantra. Her opinion mattered more than any other, she decided. She made enemies but she didn't care; she was indifferent, care-less (she could care less). She lived her life according to her own drummer, her friends and colleagues said. Invitations to dinner parties ceased. She's insufferable everyone agreed. Had she noticed? Yes and no.

In the summer, she escaped the hot city, and packed her still definitive certainties in a case with all her other summer belongings. She was certain that she was happy, for example. She was certain that the summer would be productive. Productivity was important to her. Goals. And in the past, this had been her happiness: her work. It took up a large space among her belongings: electronic equipment, folders, books, her academic reputation. But when she started to unpack the morning after her arrival at the bungalow, uncertainty overwhelmed her. She sat down on the floor and cried. She lost her appetite. She lost her certainty about the future, hers and others. Would there be no end to wars? Was there anyone she could call?

There was a thunderstorm that night and it frightened her. In the morning, it was still raining lightly and the birds twittered. She prepared the hummingbird feeders and went behind the house to pick wildflowers.

JUNK

One day, rummaging through the garage, he found a folder with his name on it. All the contents were new to him, a piece of his sequestered history.

He didn't have much energy that day—a sleepless night, too many obligations—and the thought of revelations after so much time had passed was not welcome. But the folder was there, an accusation: *Own up.* Because, in truth, he knew what was in it, had always known. Once the folder was open, he would not be able to continue the charade of anger.

He picked up the folder and opened it. It felt alive, animate. It was a decree authored by a judge when he was six years old: *Supreme Court, State of Maine.* His father's name, his stepfather's name, the word adoption, the word denied, the word final.

THE ARRANGEMENT

It was a torpid night in summer, a storm threatening. I was sitting in a café in Paris explaining the arrangement to a young woman friend—Gisela is her name. She was eager for advice—her wedding was just days away—and I am a long married, sexually experienced woman. She had asked to meet me to have talk, her mother long deceased, and so on.

The moon was buried under clouds, the sky was bleak, bleaker in fact than the word gunmetal would suggest. Bleaker than the expression starless night, though there were no stars visible that night. I was in the midst of a love affair but I was no longer in love. I was trying to explain.

The years will pass quickly, I began, and your innocence and passion will fade. There will be an arrangement.

I knew I was being cruel when I said this, that Gisela was still ecstatic, and would never forgive me. I will see you at the wedding, she said, and walked away. A fire engine howled in the distance.

I sat for a while and finished my cigarette. The air was stifling and stale with losses.

Dear Lover Lover Lover Far Away,

I looked for you in Paris, I looked for you in Rome, I traveled to the Greek Island we loved together and now I ask you for advice about the moon and the gunmetal sky that descends in London and Paris as winter approaches and where I rest my bunions in little hotels by the water, what water does not matter—a river, an estuary, the sea. Some years have passed eventfully or uneventfully since my last communication and I have found this PO address among my chaotic belongings and I am not even certain if it is yours. Is it? If only we were still tribal, our obligations would be clear. We could not love, dear lover, and then discard.

Sincerely,

_____

APHRODITE

after a painting by Botticelli

One day, as she was emerging from the foamy bath and standing in front of him with her eyelids pulled back, the retinas exposed, he spoke of his decision. There was nothing between them but the puddle at her feet and the abandoned shell. She backed away, the sea at her back, the shell's scalloped edge cutting her heels. His face was stone, emptied of love.

She asked, "Why has Apollo chosen this moment to return me to the sea?"

But he did not reply.

She swam to the horizon and then beyond. Her wounded heart, a viscous fluid, once again became a jelly fish.

Carpe Diem

What We Learn from Cranes

Wait until low tide before stepping out onto the estuary. Walk slowly and with attention to the muddy ground. Remain light of foot. Turn away from the setting sun and then back again into its cooling rays. Rest in the grasses along the embankment. Take flight as the tide returns.

A COMFORTING STORY

Welcome to another comforting story. The setting: a sun which is a red ball flaring over the western sky beyond the mountains. There was a storm earlier in the day and storm clouds are still visible in the distance. We are driving to the mall which is in a valley surrounded by cliffs and there are birds riding the updrafts over the tree line, the mountains and forests dense with life. Hikers are sitting in their cars waiting for the storm's final retreat and deer are crouching under bushes. Two baby raccoons are splattered on the road and their spirits are playing in the wind. You remember the dead snake on the porch and the felled birch tree still fresh with sap on the other side of the retaining wall, how you sat on that wall with friends sucking on the whittled branches of that tree. Pulsing and fast you grew to adulthood on that wall.

MOUNTAINTOP

I would like to feel the top of a mountain, to inhale deeply the sweet thin air and fly in the updraft of a glacier's path. My lover is on top of the mountain. He sheds his clothes and falls backwards into the stars. I build a house on top of the mountain with no boundaries and no inflections, rooms opening to the heart of the earth. By midnight I am throbbing like a toad's throat. This is my mountain top of supple flesh and sparkling tears, soft as a newborn's touch.

A Story About a Lamp

I was carrying a simple, blue, ceramic lamp down the street. The lamp had a big, round bottom and a white shade tipping one way and then another way in the wind. I held the bottom with one hand and the shade with the other and kept walking. I was pleased I'd thought to remove the bulb, but still annoyed by the wind and the lamp's awkwardness.

It was rush hour and the street was crowded. I heard a voice say, "Excuse me," but didn't know where it was coming from. Then again, "Excuse me," very persistent and desperate, I thought. Was it a beggar, one of the homeless vagabonds that sleep on the church stoop opposite by apartment building and haunt the neighborhood? Then I felt someone at my back. I spun around and almost hit her with the lamp.

It was a woman wearing a pink scarf. She had white hair and her face was cherubic, her expression sane.

"Where did you get that lamp, if you don't mind my asking?"

She spoke softly with a slight accent.

"Are you British?" I asked.

That would have made her even more sane and attractive to me. Luckily she said, "yes."

"Well, do you remember Conran's?" I asked.

"Oh yes," she said. "Is it from there?"

"Years ago when I lived in London," I said.

"Oh well," she said. "Everything has too much decoration these days. I want something plain."

"Yes, plain. Plain indeed," I said, thinking of the ways in which I was divesting to simplify my life.

111

Then there was a pause. The wind was blowing and it was cold. The woman with the pink scarf looked longingly at the lamp. It was though she had stepped out of my past to claim me and, for an instant, I wanted to give her the lamp in recognition of this, but I had promised the lamp to my daughter.

One way or another, it wasn't mine any more. I had passed it on.

XI

ZA

EL

EM

DO RE MI FA SO LA TI DO

SNOW

Wet ground covers the bear's den at the back of the garden. I say to myself: if only the snow would stop, if only the sun would rise. All this at three in the morning.

False spring, he had appeared briefly, his dark hair matted with twaddle and spit. He swatted at the squirrel foraging under the bird feeder, then found last summer's nest, the remnants of cardinal's eggs, the snowman's carrot nose, its lower body blanketed in drift.

Dogs howl like coyotes, coyotes like dogs. A family of chipmunks rattle the eaves, a snake is curled under the belly of the cold wood stove. Down by the farm an old man, a neighbor, a friend, emerges from a self-imposed hibernation reluctant to speak. In the distance, just over his right shoulder, the frozen groundhogs lie prostrate inside their tunnels. He steps on them in his dreams and hears them pop. Keep walking to the pond, he says, collect the pods as mulch, remove your shoes as you enter the mudroom and wipe what you have seen from your mind. There is no way to stop the snow or shift the season, no way to return to sleep. Even a poet's words are impotent against the searing wind and the ice particles forming on the wilted geraniums.

Now comes the junco with his black upper body chirping his winter song and the red-bellied woodpecker sounding like a whale. Why do some seasons feel too short and others too long? They arrive and we complain, vanquished by nature and nature's intention.

Remembering a Recipe
with Dannon Yogurt

Red lettering on a white ground in a waxed container about the size of a coffee cup. No need to decant the luscious contents. Eat a few bites and then add a chopped peeled carrot. Crunch and slurp.

Symphony

We were walking across the reservoir at mid-day into the bald eagle preserve and we were quiet and kept moving, as the sign instructed. Bold black letters on a yellow ground, covered in plastic, the sign didn't belong in the preserve, we thought. These precious birds, everyone knew they were nesting up in the highest tree, mountains on all sides, a steep embankment, driftwood along the edges. The preserve was a cathedral of hope and we were reverent without a sign telling us to be reverent. We knew what awaited us if we remained patient. We walked slowly and then we rested on a quarried rock, white with brown flecks. There were four of us; no one spoke.

The tallest pine on the peninsula held the nest, visible to the naked eye. We spotted a bird, but said nothing. We didn't shout, or point, or remonstrate. The bird was flying and we could see it clearly: a white head, long legs grasping a chipmunk or a mouse. It wasn't as big as we'd imagined, but it was grand, gliding past us, indifferent to us, like a teenager strutting his stuff.

It will always remain a mystery why the eagle flew so close to us that day. It was like listening to a symphony that echoes within us for the rest of our lives.

Water to water dust to dust stopping on water as we must.

Whose waves they are we think we know the riptides flow beneath us slow.

We stand aloft we stop and go as riptides flow beneath us slow.

All together now: Water to water dust to dust stopping on water as we must.

ON THE GREEN

You're walking along the golf course towards the sound—
you and your golfing friends—early spring, late afternoon,
fading light, and there's an old man on a bed in the middle of
the green waiting for you. His hair is white and so is his skin
and he continually rises from the bed to putt and swing.
Some say it's a miracle he is still alive and still golfing. He
needs a caddy but there are none available, they have all
disappeared, so he waits for you as his last recourse, the only
person on the green who might be willing to carry his clubs.
He smiles as you approach and you think: He looks familiar
but what is he doing here? The old man is singing, bursting
with story and song. You can hear the words clearly: *Play
on.*

In the beginning, everything is want: a devouring sea, a suckling breast, desire. Later, the skin enclosing our body tires. We are vexed.

Trust the wind. Slide with the curling wave as it pours onto a sandy beach, pebble and shells rattling like a turtle smiling at dawn.

Trust the wind. Do not retreat into redoubts and caves. Rise into the flickering light. Observe the dragonfly's wings. Observe a buttercup.

NOMADS 2

Urban Myths

THE FRENCH AMBASSADOR
TAKES A MISTRESS

Last night Louise, my neighbor on the floor above, entertained the French Ambassador in her kitchen. It's a small kitchen, plants on the windowsill, spices in a rack on the wall—a working kitchen in other words—but a small one. And did I mention that we have cockroaches in our building and the occasional mouse? So I said to Louise, not that she asked, I said to her that the kitchen is no place to entertain an ambassador. And she said to me, *Chéri* (practicing her French), do not worry, I know what I am doing.

I am not naive *n'est ce-pas*? I knew that eventually *le petit tête-à-tête* would drift to other rooms in Louise's apartment. And so it happened. I was watching my favorite television program and suddenly I heard a dog barking. Louise does not own a dog. In fact, none of my neighbors own dogs. And soon after the bark, I heard a scream, and then the click of a dog's paws on the bare wooden floor and a door slamming.

Then all was quiet. *Alors* what had happened? I tried to continue watching my program but could not concentrate.

EVALUATING A DANCER

You have been called upon to evaluate a dancer though you have no experience or inclination. Monday morning, early, you find yourself in a studio with long-limbed, tense-muscled young women. They are dancing without accompaniment in tandem with one another. There is no pattern, no choreography; each dancer is a soloist.

There is a piano, shrouded in a white sheet, and you wonder what has happened to the pianist. Is she delayed? Is he ill? Has s/he disappeared?

It is a bright day and, as the sun rises, it blinds you. Yet, you are here to look. You put on your sun scopes. Your task is to examine the dancers philanthropically as they slide across your field of vision. You are sitting on a floating throne that hovers above the dancers' heads, or just next to them.

And then, suddenly, all is quiet, all is still. The dancers collapse onto the floor to stretch. The click of their toe shoes on the floor ceases. The sun shifts and the room darkens. The throne on which you sit settles.

LIPS

The Mexican musicians get on the train at 145th and there's an audible sigh as they interrupt the solitude and serenity of the long ride, and people put down their newspapers, or shut their books, or look up and down and up again. I bookmark what I am reading on my electronic reader, hold my ears, and study lips. Thin lips, thick lips, puckered lips, sloppy lips. The musicians are mostly handsome, dressed like cowboys and have nice soft thick lips. But they shouldn't be on the train and I am really annoyed so I continue looking at everyone's lips. Lips, lips, lips, I say to myself. This inventory takes my mind off the irritation I feel because I have no intention of giving the musicians any money which would mean I'd have to take my hands off my ears, dig into my purse for loose coins or a dollar bill—most people give dollar bills I notice—and I have no intention of exposing my open purse or, for that matter, the embarrassing disorganization of my purse. And how could I do this when I am holding my ears anyway?

Please understand, it isn't that I don't like the music or want to help these handsome Mexican musicians, but I don't want to listen to them unless I want to listen to them, or choose to listen to them, and I don't appreciate being trapped in a subway car with them clacking their instruments, walking up and down, and up and down, hat in hand. It doesn't seem fair and really don't they know that it is illegal? And if they are illegal, doing something illegal isn't such a good idea, is it?

From time to time I wonder if I should turn them in. Someone has to do it, I say to myself. But I never do. I just hold my ears and continue to study lips.

BEAUTIFUL PEOPLE

I stood near the doors watching everyone. I had been homeless for three weeks, riding the subways, begging for food. I thought it would be hard to ask for food and I was right. It was hard. Once or twice I thought I might be hurt, even killed. Can you spare me a dollar, can you spare me some food? That's all I said. I didn't apologize for interrupting, I just said it. I didn't wish everyone a good day or bless them. I just walked slowly down the length of the car and begged. And I tried to maintain my dignity. I hoped I didn't smell too bad.

I remembered the photos I'd studied about the 1930s—breadlines, apple carts, so many people out of work. How is it different now?

If I tell you that I have a college education would you believe me? If I tell you that I have never had a drug in my life, or stolen anything, would you believe me? If I told you I once owned a bungalow on the Jersey shore would you believe me? That I grew up in a nice house? Had a good job? That I have no children and no family?

Once, a long time ago, running around the reservoir with a friend, he commented that all the beautiful people in New York were running around the reservoir that day, that they would go home and shower in their beautiful apartments and set out for their beautiful jobs and eat dinner in beautiful restaurants and send their beautiful children to beautiful private schools. And we are one of them, he said, we are beautiful too, we've made it.

AN ENCOUNTER WITH
AN OPERA SINGER

We could have been in Rome or Paris or Berlin, walking in the gardens, gardens with statues and fountains. It might have been spring, the air moist with blossom and seed. Perhaps a light rain had been falling all morning and I was sauntering under my cheerful turquoise umbrella. I was not going anywhere in particular, I had no errands, no destination. The gravel path was fresh and crunched under my new leather shoes. I was wearing a patterned dress and he was walking behind me, humming. I turned around and said, "You are singing." And he said, "One must not stop singing."

He was carrying groceries and when I saw the chard escaping from his bag, the large leaves with their red veins drooping over and nearly falling out, I began to laugh. And I said, "I see you have bought some vegetables." And he said, "One must not stop eating vegetables."

And as he talked, it was as though he was singing. I asked if he was a singer. "A baritone," he said.

He was tall and slim, wearing a black jacket. And though his hair was dyed black with gray showing at the roots, he was ageless, like other angels I have met.

AT THE DINER

The man behind the counter has owned the diner for twenty-eight years. He's very handsome—Greek—white hair, sculpted features, lapis eyes, and a blue linen shirt open one button too many. He's talking to a woman sitting two stools down, giving her advice about love and marriage. "First comes love, then comes marriage," she says. It's an old tune and the handsome Greek diner owner doesn't like it. I can see him scowl behind the hair draped flirtatiously over his right eyebrow. "I tried that" he says. "Three times."

Then comes the advice. "Are you being realistic, a woman of your age?" he asks. "Do you think you deserve what you are longing for?" And so on.

The woman doesn't seem insulted. She doesn't ask for her check or leave without paying her check. She answers the owner's rhetorical questions, more or less. I am thinking that she wants him, that this is a game they play whenever she sits at the counter and orders her diner food. Or maybe they are lovers. Yes, I think they may be lovers.

I order a poached egg on toast from one of the waiters and a vanilla ice cream soda. For some reason I am craving the soda; the egg is for nourishment. And now I am enjoying myself at the counter; I feel free. And just as I am enjoying my solitude and the conversation about love and marriage to my left, the owner comes over and asks if everything is okay. "Yes it is," I say and return to sipping the ice cream soda.

"No one has ordered an ice cream soda at 10 in the morning before," the owner says.

Despite his good looks, he is a bit gruff, not my type at all, and why is he coming on to me? After all, the woman next to me, a woman of a certain age, has been trying to hold his attention. He has been stringing her along and now he is talking to me.

"Advice is an extra service I provide," he says.

"Oh is that on the menu?" I ask. "Free advice? Unsolicited advice?"

"It can be," he says, and winks.

"Do you wink at all your customers?" I ask.

"Let me get your check," he says.

Meanwhile the woman next to me, who obviously craves the owner as much as I have been craving an ice cream soda, looks close to tears. I pick up my check—which has arrived quickly, I might add—lean over and say to her: "End it now."

She smiles. Maybe she is even grateful. I hope so.

THE LOST BRIEFCASE

Dear Madam,

I am happy to inform you that we have found your brief-case. As reported, you had left it in the airport lounge, Gate 23, Domestic Terminal. One of our responsible cleaning staff has retrieved it and placed it in our hands.

For your information, the briefcase contains: an iPad, a small notebook nearly filled with black-inked handwritten notes, an envelope addressed to you with typed pages and two pens. The notes, Madam, reminded me of my school days.

We are sorry you went to the trouble of locking your iPad. We opened it and found the words, "This is a lost iPad." We are trustworthy and most of our staff is bonded. As for the notebook, we found many of the entries intriguing though there was little or no identification of its author or subjects. We wondered why this might be the case Are you on the run? Is this why you were careless enough to leave your briefcase behind as you were about to embark on your journey? We hope, sincerely, that your trip was not disrupted by your loss. And we are deeply sorry for your temporary loss.

Kindly report to the Lost & Found in the terminal at your earliest convenience. Bring ID.

Sincerely,

The Lost and Found

Dear Sir,

Thank you for your letter of last Thursday. I am grateful that you took such great care with my briefcase and tried to locate me. It might have been simple if you looked at the address label on the envelope. But you did not. Instead, you opened my iPad and looked inside my journal. Who gave you this authority, sir? At the very least, an apology is in order when I come to retrieve my briefcase, or in writing, at your earliest convenience.

Yours sincerely,

Dear Madam,

We have the authority as vested in us.

Sincerely yours,

THE MAN WHISTLING ON THE A

The man nodded and huddled closer to the girl with the mousey hair. She'd taken off her hat and her hair was straggly and looked unwashed. She turned her back on him as best she could but her left hip and breast were touching his arm. He moved it up and down, up and down. It was hard to tell if she was upset, or timid, or flattered. There was no expression on her face, but she had begun to sweat. She said nothing. No one else on the train said anything either.

The train was crowded, the day of the incoming storm, the biggest we have ever seen, the Mayor said, inciting a panic among New Yorkers. Within minutes, there was nothing left on the shelves. A man with a large bottle of Poland Spring lodged between his feet held tightly to the pole next to the woman. He was reading his e-reader, ignoring the man touching-up the woman.

Everyone was headed home early from work before the transit shutdown, and if the electricity went down before that, the train would stop and that bottle of Poland Spring water would be the only water for many hours, more than likely. And would this man who was so close to the woman with straggly hair, the woman who was being man-handled, would he share his water?

All of these contingencies, all of this drama, did not stop the offending man from getting closer to the girl. The train stopped in the tunnel before 59th to let the D train pass, and then it lurched forward again tipping the man's body full frontal into the woman. He began to whistle. He had his headset on, maybe reggae, maybe rock, hard to tell, didn't matter. His eyes were closed, he was bopping and weaving and touching the girl. There was no room to move away and the woman was stuck facing the whistling man. He was whistling for her.

CAIRO BUTTONS

It was a hot summer in Cairo, hotter than usual. The streets were dusty and crowded. He was on business, dressed in a powder-blue linen suit, a straw hat and a bow tie.

He could have been on the streets of New York, so stylish was he that year. A young man, recently graduated from a prestigious school, employed by a prestigious bank right out of college.

He had taken the assignment in Cairo without complaint; heat did not agree with him. He had only been there a month when, unconcerned for his safety or the eccentricity of his appearance in the Cairo streets, he walked into a busy intersection and was hit by a bicycle. He was taken to a hospital where his leg was amputated. Under anesthetic, he called out for his mother. The surgeon found this amusing, and when the young man woke up, he told him what he had said. But the young man did not understand his strong accent.

After several weeks of convalescence, an under-secretary from the embassy arrived to arrange for his passage home. The bank had agreed to pay. Needless to say, the young man was relieved and grateful. His life had been upended before it had barely begun.

Once on board the liner, he wondered what had gone wrong, and whether he had been careless, thus causing his own accident. Was this possible? If so, what had he been thinking about when he stepped out into the intersection? And then he remembered. That very morning two buttons had come loose: one on his trouser pocket, the other on the sleeve of his shirt.

He had always believed that bad things happen in threes. He should have been more attentive, he thought, and fixed the buttons before he left his apartment.

HAVE YOU EVER BEEN THERE?

A young woman with her son on her lap is sitting next to an old woman on the Fifth Avenue bus. It is rush hour and there are many tourists in town; the young woman is a tourist. The old woman is on her way to meet a friend who lives all the way downtown. She doesn't usually take the Fifth Avenue bus in the summer—too many tourists.

Traffic. The bus driver is aggravated and asking people to please move to the back of the bus. "Please. Please move to the back of the bus." They have now been at the stop too long and the crowd is restive.

"Are you having a good time?" the old woman asks.

"Yes. A very good time."

"And where are you staying?"

"Brooklyn."

Her English is okay but limited. One, two-word, three-word word answers with a hesitation between each word, trying to find the word.

"And where are you from?"

"Austria. Have you ever been there?"

Now that is an interesting question for the old woman, but she doesn't say anything. Once she begins to talk about her Viennese family there's no stopping her. They were murdered in the camps. Nazi genocide. She hardly utters these words any more.

What does this young woman know? Maybe something. Maybe everything. Maybe nothing. 70-years ago, the old woman says to herself, everyone dead and forgotten. Why should I spoil this young woman's holiday and make this annoying bus ride even worse.

"Salzburg, Vienna," the old woman says. "I've been to Salzburg and Vienna."

"Beautiful, *nicht*?" the young woman says.

"Beautiful," the old woman says.

LITTLE NELL'S NIGHTMARE

In the event she was lost and the sky was turbulent, garbage strewn here and about under the scaffolding at King's Cross whereupon she huddled in a doorway and was found. But she was not in London, she was in China standing atop the Great Wall all lonesome and undefended. Whereupon an army of men with hard faces and shallow chins descended upon her, not for the purpose of rescue, but for the purpose of incarceration inside a cave. "If you would leave off vexing me it would please me, dearly," Little Nell said when they allowed her to speak. But they did not understand, not at all. And she did not understand them either.

OOH MAN, DIG THAT CRAZY CHICK

My heart exploded when my parents said I could travel to New York with my friends. We had just graduated from high school and all of us had plans for the summer—mostly working—to help pay for our tuitions. I had been hired by a camp in Ontario as a junior counselor. I had never been to Canada or anywhere very far from where I grew up and I wanted an adventure.

We were poor girls from a small town on the New Jersey-Pennsylvania border. But we were also smart girls; all of us were headed to college. We did the usual girlie things—lots of gossip about boys, lots of talk about make-up, fashion, diets and music—but we also had ambition, ambition without much guidance from our parents who had suffered financial insecurity and other travails all of their lives. Thanks for their abiding love for us, this little coterie of girl-childs had done well. They were five of us and we had been stuck like glue since kindergarten.

On the day in question, texts were flying back and forth all morning. If we were to have a day in the city, we had to get started early. The bus left at 8 a.m. Our get-home curfew was 9 p.m. and we were more than two hours out of the city.

It was hot, into the high 90s, and everything we had planned to wear got thrown back into the closet. We decided on shorts and halter tops, sandals, and a shoulder bag filled with snacks (to save money), a water bottle, and a shirt for air conditioning.

As soon as we debarked, we knew something was wrong. The workers at Port Authority hissed and made lewd comments. Getting outside into the putrid air was a relief. We walked east towards Bryant Park and collapsed onto some rickety chairs, pulled out maps and water, and tried to get our bearings. Where was our list? What had we decided to do?

We looked around at the crowd—young and old, native and foreign. It was only the European women who looked like us, which I suppose was a compliment. We were hot—and I don't mean the temperature. We were young, sexy, smart women. We remembered that song: *Who wears short shorts?* We do.

IT'S NOT EXACTLY THE HAMPTONS

It's not exactly The Hamptons where they are spending their summer, not exactly, not even remotely does the city, where they are spending their summer, resemble The Hamptons. Friends, colleagues, even family, assume they are spending their summer in The Hamptons, where they have always spent their summers. But not this year. Not this year or in any foreseeable year, unfortunately. And fortune comes into it. Or lack thereof. And lay-offs. Both of them have been laid off. Plenty of savings, but not forever.

They don't explain or defend. They don't disabuse friends, colleagues, and family of any theories expressed about their straitened circumstances. They don't respond to pity, or humorous patronizing remarks, or stories about recent travels to Timbuktu, or a renovation of a bathroom. Once upon a time, not so long ago, they had renovated their bathroom. But now they have crashed, they are scared, they are downsized.

They remain silent, unwilling to burden their friends or family. Cheerfully, they wish everyone a good summer, an enjoyable summer, a good trip, and a successful renovation.

TEXAS

He leaned against the pole in the center of the train, his thin arm wrapped around it to steady himself as the car lurched. His girlfriend had taken a seat and he was aggravated at her, even embarrassed that she had done so. It was rush hour, they were visitors to the city, they didn't have rights. Hadn't she noticed the woman standing above her, glaring, exhausted after a day's work, her briefcase on the floor between her legs.

At the next stop, he had decided, he'd ask his girlfriend to relinquish her seat. Maybe the crowd would ease and he could inch his way over. He tried to signal to her but she was reading texts or playing a video game, oblivious to what she had done, oblivious to him.

His hometown was Lubbock, Texas where men were gentlemen and older women—married or single—were still addressed as "Ma'am."

The woman with the briefcase between her legs wasn't old—somewhere in her late forties or early fifties and he knew that city life was different, that age wasn't a signifier as it was back home, but he was in his twenties and he had a learned respect for his elders his girlfriend didn't share having grown up in Austin, a more cosmopolitan town. They were in medical school together, equals in that respect, and they were visiting the city for the first time, staying with friends in an uptown neighborhood, and using the subway.

He was a small man with a big heart. He wanted the woman who had been working all day to have a seat. He wanted his girlfriend to notice the woman and offer her the seat. He wanted his girlfriend to notice him.

BAR STORY

They tried to understand what had happened. It had happened fast, they'd been drinking—what else does one do at a bar (while socializing of course)—and talking about the descriptions of various wines on the chalk board. Someone had a good handwriting they noticed; it looked like calligraphy. Different colored chalks plus a drawing of a wine glass. Pretty damn good.

There were three of them, all men, hanging out after work. Where else was there to go? They had nothing much to talk about except their work and the descriptions of the wine and where they were going on their next vacation and their electronic devices. All three cell phones were on the bar, silenced, but lighting up now and again and demanding their attention—a tweet or a text.

A couple slid in next to them, a man and a woman, the woman much younger than the man and pretty, the man balding and overweight. The three friends began to whisper and giggle like a bunch of schoolgirls. And the balding man noticed and said, "Hey, what are you looking at?" The way he slurred his words, it was obvious he'd had a head start at another bar somewhere. But this didn't stop the three friends from hooting and howling and making lewd remarks to the woman. "That your daughter?" one of them asked.

Within seconds, fists were flying and the older balding guy was on the floor. Not surprisingly, everyone had a different story to tell the cops depending on whose side they were on—the three young guys or the balding older guy and his pretty young date—and where they were sitting at the bar. The bartender had a story, so did the manager. And then the balding man with the young date told his story and then the three guys told their story and then the young date told her story. And every story was wrong except for my story. I was there. I saw what happened.

PREACH CHRIST AND HIM CRUCIFIED

Arrival at the church on Broadway and 113th ten minutes before the concert. Saturday night after the storm. Snow dunes, slush, travel delays, wet socks inside the boots. Organ pipes imposing, dark wood paneling, church dating to austere 1850s, Presbyterian. Meaning what exactly? Cellist and pianist rehearsing: Bach, Martinu, Brahms. Videocam set up, pews filling, laughter. Mostly musicians, friends, friends of musicians.

The Martinu is Nuevo Tango, the Brahms is Jazz. The audience is mesmerized, alert, blasphemous in its lust for more music. Handel for the encore, more sedate, so we can slide back into the syncopated city in a more reverent mood.

Sunday morning sermon. Because He died (capital "H"), all is forgotten, all forgiven.

LISTENING TO CHET BAKER

Late at night and sometimes all night. The radio on, the station so nearby there is never any static. The only static is outside the door of her bedroom: parents arguing, doors slamming, kid sister crying. Then quiet, the sound of a bus, a siren in the distance and Chet Baker on his horn. The phone rings, a black rotary phone. She remembers the number: Atwater 9-8835. *Baby, sing the blues.* Her boyfriend has stopped calling. Who would be calling at this hour?

"Baby are you wearing underwear?" the voice asks. Her boyfriend is chaste compared to this vulgar man. Why is he so chaste?

"Didn't I tell you not to list your number?" her mother says the first time this happened. "All those perverts out there."

The street is a Hopper painting, late at night, shadowy figures behind venetian blinds, shadows falling across a desk, a bed, a dresser. A man across the street is watching her, 3 a.m. and she can't sleep. He's exposing himself. She pulls down the shade all the way, street lights casting more shadow. Why do these men—the whispering men, the exposing men—why do they only want to touch themselves?

She turns up the volume on the radio, a whole night of Chet. He promises something else, something more: languorous candlelit dinners, seduction, love.

A PAINTING INSIDE A PAINTING

Love inside love, a painting inside a painting, a city inside a city. She bought flowers: hyacinth and tulips. It was spring.

Big love inside big love, a long road through bumpy terrain. A tuned-up engine inside an engine.

He offered lunch.

A wild exactitude, he said.

She agreed and said:

This love inside love, this painting inside a painting, this city inside a city, this story inside a story.

GERMAN SKY

They stopped to speak to a Romanian friend married to a Russian woman. It was an end-of-winter day, still cold but sunny, and the sky was cloudless. They found the sunniest spot near the traffic circle at the entrance to the park and talked and talked. About the end of winter, about work, about the feral cats living in the park. Had they survived the winter? They were enjoying the sun and the intimation of spring on a day that was sunny and cloudless and not quite spring. The Romanian friend looked up and said, "This is a German sky." His parents had suffered a German-occupied Romania so how could a bright sunshiny day—cold and clear—be German so many years after the war ended? The liminal sky, the sheltering sky, the sky that caresses and protects us.

"How can this be a German sky?" someone asked.

"It was a German sky before the Russians came in. After that, it was a Russian sky," the Romanian said.

His Russian wife smiled. Her sky was Russian.

MTF

You approach me as though we have been friends for a very long time. You want my opinion about the chairs. You covet the chairs.

I have just entered the thrift store and you are there beside me,—tall, lean, elegant in a white fitted summer suit. Your blouse is coral matching your lipstick and your nail polish. But why are you on a walker, the walker loaded down with packages on its handles?

"I've just had back surgery," you explain. "But I'm doing fine."

You are interested in the Ottoman in the window and three chairs. One of them has interesting carvings and you point to them with your long fingers. It is only then I realize that your features are large—your hands, your nose, your lips—and that your voice has an odd timbre that slides in and out of different registers and that you are wearing a wig.

You want the Ottoman, you want the chairs, but alas they are not going on sale until tomorrow and it would mean returning at 8 a.m.

"Is that too early for you?" I ask.

It's a very personal question but somehow I am unashamed. This woman and I are old friends. We've just had lunch together and now we are on a shopping spree.

"You must live in a large apartment to accommodate so much furniture," I say.

"Oh no, dear, I live in a studio."

"A large studio?"

"Large enough," you say.

"And you must be a performer?"

147

"Some have said so."

"Those gestures, your voice, your elegance."

"It takes one to know one, dear."

PAUL

on our 50th anniversary

He was a real alive person with a strange last name. I could not spell it. I never met him formally, he was just there. After, we never had a phone call, much less a rendezvous anywhere in the world. I followed him. I was a groupie. I worked shifts, I took any work I could get, I was a dog's body.

I was twelve-years-old when he came to New York for his first concert. My mother bought me the LIFE magazine with the photo spread of his visit, including the hysterical girls screaming behind the barrier in front of his hotel. "I am glad this isn't you," my mother said. She didn't know I was there.

I didn't tell anyone I was in love with Paul McCartney—not the Beatles, just him—though I wrote him secret love letters in my diary. It was a pink leatherette diary with a lock. I kept it locked. I kept myself locked.

And then one day when I was in college and still living at home, I saw him walking down Fifth Avenue and I followed him. I wanted to say something to him, but what? "I love you, Paul?" or "I love your music, Paul." That wasn't true. I didn't love the music, I loved him. No one else seemed to recognize him until he crossed the street and ambled into Rockefeller Center. He was alone, wearing a long dark blue coat—a standard celebrity costume I have learned—the collar pulled up to his nose, no hat, though it was a blustery cold day. He walked over to the ice skating rink and watched the skaters for a while. The tree was already up and the lights turned on as we stood there, more or less side by side, like old friends, or lovers. I wanted to reach for his hand but hesitated, one of my many regrets.

WHAT DID I DO WRONG?

The streets are clean and people wait at the stop lights, no jay-walking, not much talking in the street. Yet here I am, settled, married, having given up my waywardness, my mischievous smile and all else that identifies me as a happy American male from a privileged background, the Chicago burbs where my family still lives. Needless to say, they are shocked at my situation. "Is it any better than being imprisoned?" my lawyer father asked me. That's one question. As for my mother, she has a different one: "What did we do wrong?"

No jobs in America for a WASP PhD, yes I am a "Doctor," so I took a university position in Singapore five years ago. An adventure, all of Asia to explore. Now I have a Singaporean wife. What did I do wrong? I ask myself. Short answer: I wanted sex. She got pregnant, we got married. This is Singapore. She comes from a prominent family, no discussion. And the hard thing is—all the money in their world or mine can't fix this.

How is it possible to get stuck in a country at peace, an affluent peaceful, albeit tyrannical country in the 21st century? The answer must be embedded in the question. And just asking it gives me heart: my mind is still working, thank you.

Aren't there some international laws preventing punishment for my transgression? I say "my" because I am solely responsible, I know that. My wife is perfectly happy.

THE TORSO DREAMS

For eleven months of the year she loved the city. But then came the summer with the humidity, the tourists, and the debris. Not that the city was ever clean. During her years in European cities, she marveled at the cleanliness, the men and women hosing down the sidewalks in the mornings, sweeping in the afternoons. Was it too much to ask?

The nightmares began a year after her return. At first these dreams seemed humorous, but as they continued, they slowly, incrementally, began to feel ominous. Like a soldier returned from war, she imagined threat. She screamed and startled, trembled and wept. Her lovers went home to spend the remainder of the night in their own beds.

At a certain point, however, as she acclimated to the challenges of her new life, the nightmares became benign dreams again and she woke up laughing. The funniest were the torso dreams, a repeating narrative about mannequins in a shop window on Fifth Avenue. They had no legs or arms and were cut off at the waist. But they were clearly women. Some of them wore black short-sleeved starched shirts with high collars and plunging necklines exposing the cleavage of large breasts. Others wore red and white striped long-sleeved starched shirts with the same high collars and plunging necklines.

At the end of these dreams she went into the fashionable store and bought both of these shirts. One was for daytime wear, the other for night, she was told. But she couldn't decide which was which.

There was only one solution: wear them both, one on top of the other. Depending on the weather and her mood, she could alternate which shirt to put on top, which on the bottom. This was the sale-person's suggestion, a good one.

THE GOODBYE PARTY

I am in the Ansonia cafe, a Sunday, and it is crowded. I am there with my friend Lucinda who is moving to Mexico—permanently. Is she blissfully free-spirited, as she was when she was young, or insane? She is leaving behind furniture, friends, and an ex-husband, former lovers, children, grandchildren (albeit adopted) and, most importantly (and if you are a New Yorker you will understand this), most importantly, a rent-controlled apartment.

In walks Manhattan, opera singer—soprano. Who has a stage name like this? She's a diva, larger than her life or ours.

Can she join us? Of course. "Did you know I was moving to Mexico?"

"Well I knew you had a house there. For how long?"

"For the duration."

"The duration of what?"

Manhattan is young, vibrant, ambitious, up-and-coming. She doesn't get this.

"My dear..." Lucinda says, trailing off, like the ellipsis I have used here.

What is she looking forward to, I ask, eager to change the subject.

"The sun, the sea, my garden, a quiet life."

That I can understand.

In walks a tall man with a loping step. He is disheveled, perhaps even homeless, but no, he orders something, sits at an adjacent table, pulls out a fat notebook and begins to write, his face close to the page, a near-sighted person without spectacles.

"He's my roommate." Manhattan explains. And she waves to him but doesn't invite him over. I'm relieved. This is good-bye party and I don't want any more strangers at the table.

"Lucinda, I will miss you," I say. "I am sorry we didn't see more of each other over the years."

"Me too," she says.

"Me too," says Manhattan.

RUNNING INTO ROBBIE

On the quiet Sunday street, I run into Robbie. We used to live in the same building. He got evicted, end of story. And now here he is. Though it is winter, he is wearing a cotton shirt, a baseball cap with the visor turned to the back of his shaved head, and sandals. He's lost his teeth, his once fleshy cheeks, his jacket, his dignity. There are missing words in his sentences, his hands are trembling, he's been living on the streets and in the park for many months. His dog is dead, his girlfriend is in jail. No, please, don't call 911. They tell me I will be safe, but I am not safe, he says. I pull out my phone and call 911. The cops arrive, two big tall blonde healthy looking guys. They are kind, gentle as they take Robbie away.

THE ORIGINS OF CAPITALISM

It was strange to see the woman from Bhutan on a street in a city so far away from Bhutan, thousands of miles away, thousands and thousands of miles away. She was wearing western clothes but her face and her hair was from Bhutan. She was lost and asked the stranger for directions. He was headed the same way so they walked together. She was on her way to an interview for a nanny job, she said, and had never been to this neighborhood. Was it a nice neighborhood? She was living in Queens with some friends. No family here? he asked. No family, she said, as they continued walking and talking.

He wanted to know about her family. My husband is working in Bhutan, she said, but my children are at school out of the country. One is in medical school in Sri Lanka, the other in agricultural school in Thailand. I work here as a nanny to pay for their education. And when was the last time you were home? he asked. Five years, she said. And that was the last time you saw your husband? Yes, she said.

Her expression was happy, she had a happy face and a warm smile. How could she be so happy, the man wondered.

It's a comfort knowing I can pay for my children's education, she said, as if to answer his silent question. But I am nervous about getting this job. Thank you for walking with me.

This is where I live, he said, pointing to the street where he lives. He did not want to say goodbye.

I feel as though I have known you a long time even though it has just been a few minutes since we began walking and talking, the woman said.

If your spirit is calm you will get the job, the man said. How did he get this idea? He sounded like a man from Bhutan.

The woman laughed. You sound like my brother, she said.

The children will love you, the man said. You will get the job. I know it.

AND SUDDENLY YOU ARE IN PARADISE

You wake up and suddenly the city has disappeared, you are in paradise. You can speak French fluently, you have three grandchildren visiting you that very afternoon for tea. (They cannot wait to see you.) You can paint and draw, you attract men despite your age. (They like your breasts <u>and</u> your brain.) Your wardrobe is exotic though not particularly fashionable. (You never have a problem choosing what to wear.) And, needless to say, you are immortal.

Tall Tales

DEMOISELLE

for Picasso's women

His gaze was strong—*fuerta*. He looked at me. Angry and restless, S*ignor*, that is how I would describe him. Our assignations took place twice a month in the corner room upstairs. It is the darkest room in the house. *Stop the sun*, he said, as he entered the room and then entered me. From behind like a bull. A famous painter, you say? That is nothing to me.

If only he had requested another but he liked the young ones. Did he hurt the little one? I am not surprised, *Signor*. We must not talk back the Madam told us and the little one talked back. This bull, this small man with a big chest, he was strong—*fuerta*—and demanding.

Only later I learned that he had a wife and children and that the wife forced him to move away to the south, away from all temptation, where the sun is blinding. There, he could not close out the light or hide in darkened rooms with young whores, so he returned to Paris alone.

A famous painter, you say? That is nothing to me.

THE HEAT WAVE

For the second time in as many days he was soft and she was dumb and it was hot, so hot. He could not breathe, he was having nightmares. There was no air conditioning. It was before air conditioning, before cities, before chestnuts and bonfires, before war, before pesticides. It was dark and still early in the dark. She was next to him, her eyes flickering under her stitched lids. Come back, come back, he shouted to her. It is 77 degrees, the heat wave has broken, he said. There were no instruments to measure the temperature. He could not prove that it had cooled. He got out of bed and he was choking. The wax, hot as lava, was melting into the ground. So how could he say that it had cooled? It had not.

THE MIND RESISTS ATROCITY

Did he cut off his penis? Isn't this what everyone wants to know? We're not talking about circumcision here, we're talking about amputation. Voluntary amputation.

THINGS I HAVE STOLEN

1. A small brown plastic western horse with a white mane, no saddle, no rider. This was in nursery school and it was nap time. I was sleeping on a cot next to a boy who had a lot of these little toys. Girls were supposed to have dolls in those days. I wanted a plastic horse. He slept, I watched the horse. And then I took it. I have no idea where I put it, or if I took it home, or if I hid it, or played with it, or showed it off to my friends.

I suppose now I can say that I am unrepentant. The little boy had many horses. I had just one.

2. The Lord of the Rings from WH Smith in London. I have no idea what prompted me to steal this particular book which was large and unwieldy. I wasn't even interested in it and I don't like the genre.

I had just arrived in London for a year of study abroad and was settling in. It was gray, misty, the kind of weather I had read about in 19th century British novels but never experienced in sunny California. It wasn't cozy or moody, it was grim.

I was on my own one afternoon and feeling lost. More than lost, displaced. My boyfriend at the time was in graduate school and he was already having a love affair with someone else. I found out about it by accident—how else does one find out about love affairs—and didn't know what to do about it. We had committed to living abroad at the same time, but as soon as we debarked in Southampton, he began to ignore me. We lived in separate digs and hardly saw each other. I was bereft and ashamed. How could I have trusted him? Had I ever loved him? These were the same questions a courageous Mary Wollstonecraft asked Gilbert Imlay, her lover and the father of her child, in 1795. So much for vindication.

That's the backstory to the day I stole the book, a book I didn't want to read. I slipped it into my bag and walked out of the store. No one stopped me, no beeps went off. The next day I wanted to return it but didn't know how to do it. So I left it on a bus.

I WANTED TO BE A BRECK GIRL

Whenever I washed my hair the spell was broken. The only way to retrieve it was to step into the shower each morning and wash my hair again. I was obsessed: I wanted to be a Breck Girl.

Let me explain.

I was just twenty-one, graduated from college, looking for a job. I'd boomeranged back home and I wasn't happy. My parents were more than annoyed with me; they were unforgiving about my low grade point average. They had expected me to do better. I had expected me to do better. But I got distracted at college; I fell in love. Not with a boy, oh no, not that, I fell in love with myself, with my hair, with the possibility that my long, dark, thick hair would land me a photo session as a Breck Girl. Oh, yes. That is what I wanted. I wanted it more than anything. More than a husband, more than a fancy house, more than children.

Listen, it was the 1950s. Women didn't have much more ambition.

It was heavily scented shampoo and, truth be told, I didn't like the scent. But it lathered up quickly no matter the hardness or softness of the water. It was sunshine yellow. It was viscous. That was a good word to use at my interview, I thought.

So I applied.

ONCE UPON A TIME

One upon a time she was a cheerleader. Yes, a cheerleader. Hard to imagine, I know. Grandma, is that you?

And we began to giggle.

Another photo from that time: she had a cigarette in one hand, a champagne glass in the other.

What about this one? I asked.

And we giggled again.

Tell me about being a cheerleader, Grandma.

Well, it began like this. I was new to the school. I came in at 10th grade and everyone knew everyone. I wanted to fit in, to be popular. I was an athlete but the teams had already been formed—basketball, volleyball, softball—so I signed up to be a cheerleader. I wanted to be seen. I wanted a boyfriend.

I had no clue about being a cheerleader. None. The other girls had big boobs and little waists. I had little boobs and I was lean, a runner, a hitter. But the coach said, okay, reluctantly. I was ostracized before I even began.

We had to wear our little outfits at practice. They were expensive so the coach found me a hand-me-down. White sweater with a big T stitched on the front, a little navy blue skirt, mid-thigh, shoes and socks were up to me.

They put me at the end of the line. I learned the moves: chest out, jump in the air, rah rah rah. Rah rah rah rah.

Now I'm giggling, Grandma.

Keep giggling, Sylvie. I only lasted a couple of months. I couldn't keep a straight face I was laughing so hard. Sure I could do the moves. But I wanted to be on the field hitting the ball, any ball. That's where I belonged.

POSSESSION

Once upon a time a young man was walking in the woods. He was carving out a path between the trees on a vast expanse of land that had been deeded to him by the Federal Government. Acres and acres of land that now belonged to him. He had framed the deed and put it on his mantel in the main room of his log cabin. Now that he had the property, he could send for a mail-order bride as many of his cousins had done.

It was a Friday morning in early spring. The ground was in thaw and so was the stream bed. The birds were returning from the south and the bears had emerged from hibernation. The young man took out his surveying equipment and outlined the boundaries of his land. A fox crossed his path; it was chasing a rabbit. Then a hawk took flight and circled above him.

The man thought: If I build a wall around my property, will the foxes, rabbits, hawks and bears become mine as well?

Over the next two months, the young man collected stones to make a wall. He enlisted the help of some of his neighbors who also had deeds to their property. The wall, or series of walls, was well constructed, without mortar. Rocks were piled in sculptural equilibrium; they never toppled. Until the bears walked through them.

THE STUFFING HAS COME OUT

It was spring and she was spring cleaning. She folded up the old green quilt and loaded it into the shopping cart inside a laundry bag, took it to the laundromat, and put it into a mid-sized machine for $3.25. That seemed like a bargain. She was always looking for bargains these days.

The green quilt was ready to be tossed or recycled. She'd already stitched a hole where the stuffing was coming out and duct-taped another. A wartime invention, duct tape was used to bind up ammunition. It was water resistant and strong. She used it a lot.

But all the duct tape in the world would not save the quilt. Oh, it had such a long history dating back to the early days of her marriage. When had her life started to unravel? She couldn't let go of anything these days, she was hanging on for dear life. Her twin sons were going to college—both of them on scholarship—in the fall. She already missed them. And her husband, what about him? He'd lost his job unexpectedly. And now what? That's what they were trying to figure out.

The daily tasks were a consolation. Spring cleaning, a quilt loaded up in the washing machine. But when it stopped and she pulled the quilt out, she knew it was over. There was stuffing everywhere and she couldn't save it.

ANOTHER BRITISH MURDER MYSTERY

The drumming was loud and it made me skittish. I turned on the satellite computer. What I wanted was a weather station: when would the heat break? But there was no weather station. And the heat never broke in South Sudan. Why had I forgotten this?

I was on a reprise of a mission. I'd been here about ten years before. Unending conflict and starvation. My job was to weigh the babies, put them on IV's, reassure their mothers who already looked like cadavers themselves. As in all things, apparently, there was a tipping point, and no matter what we did, too many people died.

After nightfall, we lay under netting to protect us from voracious flies, and reiterated the plots of all the murder mysteries we'd seen on TV: Foyle's War, Broadchurch. When our memories were exhausted, we read Dickens to each other. All his work contained in one volume, a life's work, a life's accomplishment. We moved from one story to another. We took turns reading. Sometimes we made love. Sometimes we drank wine. Sometimes we prayed, strange secular prayers, made-up prayers, questioning prayers. Why are we here?

TSUNAMI

for the survivors of Katrina, Fukishima, et al.

All our possessions have been emptied onto the beach. Though this was not unexpected, it was a shock. What had belonged to us, or what we thought had belonged to us, did not belong to us. The photograph albums, all water-logged, the important documents—passports, birth certificates, marriage certificates—scattered in the dunes

There is something outside that has got to come in but there is no in. Our in-sides resemble a jellyfish. Our insides are a jellyfish. We are jellyfish.

How are the trees doing? Or the sidewalk? Or the road? Or the school? How are the children doing? Where is our dog?

EXISTENTIAL CONFUSION

As a rule I can make nothing out.
Lytton Strachey in a letter
to Virginia Woolf, Sept. 27, 1908

And what did he mean by this, Mr. Strachey? What exactly did he mean? He'd been lying on the sofa in the conservatory for a week. It was spring, everything in bloom. And he was pale after a long winter indoors sitting by the fire either moping or weeping or reading if he could concentrate. He read the drafts of Virginia's stories and essays. Her brilliance was intimidating.

His moods were volatile, his letters to Virginia always hyperbolic. She understood his moods, accepted them and wrote reassuring letters in return. He might have been an actor, she had said to him. But in his privileged, rarified, upper-class childhood, there were expectations. A barrister, perhaps? His dramatic flare would have served him well at the Inns of Court. Those gowns and wigs. Or if not a barrister, perhaps Parliament? Speechifying. Yes, he could do that, he agreed.

What do you think will happen to me? he asked Virginia. But she couldn't answer. The voices in her head were obliterating her common sense.

And so he missed her and told her so. I miss you, Virginia. Please do not leave me. Please do not ever leave me.

ANGELS

They descend and ascend. They are ephemeral and ethereal. They carry light and reflect light. They take flight. They exude a scent: jasmine (female) or pomegranate (male). They taste sweet and sour. They are—by definition— angelic, one who performs healing acts and gestures without premeditation. In art and life we refer to them as blessed creatures who bless us with their presence. And when we are in their presence, we feel fortunate and blessed, though we may not know this until they have dissolved into a puddle or evaporated into a hazy fog. Oh, that was an angel, we might say, and mean it. But we cannot retrieve an angel or touch an angel. It is not possible.

THE INTRUDER

She met the journalist two days after her arrival. He was sitting in the darkened library tuning his cello before the evening's entertainment. A small spotlight shone on his long-fingered, well- manicured hands. And it was his hands that she noticed before anything else about him. Hands or lips, either way, she was in trouble.

All the residents of the artist's colony were required to perform, or entertain with a reading or memorized recitation. It was a pressured environment, not very relaxing, but good for the work they had been told during rigorous auditions.

The journalist, who was also a musician, had left his post in Istanbul to take advantage of the fellowship. He had been covering the war in Afghanistan and had brought with him a restlessness that unsettled everyone in the colony.

But his hands were beguiling. She wanted them on her. And though she feigned indifference, she manipulated an introduction. Their affair began that night.

Almost as soon as they were in his room, he offered her opium. His passion was muted and she felt no pleasure with him. She had made a mistake. It wasn't until the drug wore off nearly two days later that she understood: any felt connection with this war-struck man was an illusion. His first mistress was the pipe and always would be.

REFUGEES WITH WILD EYES

The boat had traveled in the wrong direction—west instead of east. They had been drifting for many days on the currents, on the swells. There was no food or water, they were blistered, parched. Sometimes there were stars, sometimes the sky was black, once or twice there was a storm. The raft was sturdy and for that they were grateful. An artisan from their village had built it in the cellar of his house before the soldiers arrived. And that was fortunate, fortune among so many misfortunes.

Five of them had decided to make the break together, all men, women and children left behind. We will send for you, they had said. We will not abandon you.

They were not asking permission.

A BABY BLUE CRAB

I smoothed down my mustache and stroked the underside of my chin. Maybe she would notice the dimple in my chin. I had heard she covets dimples.

"One more thing before you go," she said. "Remove the crab from the tank. Bring it to me. It will fit in the palm of your hand."

It was a baby blue crab lying on its back. Its legs moved incessantly as I held it.

"I intend to eat the crab," she said as I handed it to her.

And she pointed to the pot of boiling water on the stove.

She put the crab into the pot. It turned red. The blue had vanished and so had my dimples.

The Last Word

A NEW YORK TIMES
PRIVILEGED CHILDHOOD

There was a newspaper every morning on the mat outside their apartment door. They were on the seventh floor and this was a marvel. How did it get there and so early? They were at the breakfast table by 6:30—all four of them—and Father had opened the door and picked up the paper before they were all assembled. Being the man of the house and the most interested in domestic politics and foreign affairs—at least that was the explanation until the girls went to college and learned better—he had prerogatives on the newspaper. That said, he shared its contents by reading various articles aloud and then asking questions. These questions could be challenged, within limits. Mother listened proudly to her daughters. How did she show this pride? With her silence.

It was the eldest who challenged the *status quo*. Despite youth and ignorance, she answered questions courageously and was, in her every-day life, a disobedient adversary. Dominance and submission, a dangerous game she was willing to play from an early age. For this she was rewarded with the arts section of the newspaper. Mostly, she looked at the movie ads and advertisements. Father did not expect much more. That's very good, dear, he said, whenever his eldest daughter spoke. She drew the pages back as He did into a kind of scroll, right to left, and felt very grown up.

These days, she misses the smell of the paper, the newsprint on her hands, the small, intact family at the breakfast table tog ether, and Father's lessons about all the world's glories and woes.

WHAT PEOPLE SAY

I am so sorry you have to go through this.

It is what it is.

Your story has a lot of moving parts.

Turn the glass over.

I am sorry for your loss.

I am so sorry for your loss.

ON HOLD

Please ask our representative for more information. Let us help you prepare for a comfortable retirement. The next representative will be with you shortly. If your change jar is getting heavy, bring it in to us. Let us help you prepare for a comfortable retirement. Too much is never enough. A representative will be with you shortly.

SHE GOT WHAT SHE WANTED

After she died, but before the memorial, someone said, "she got what she wanted." They came, they went, they paid their respects, and they repeated that careworn phrase. What did it mean exactly? That she had died gradually, peacefully, relatively pain-free, her friends and family talking to her, singing to her, embracing her? Is that what she wanted? What about the drama of a terminal illness for a woman with very young children, still young herself, or the day the doctor announced that she had three months to live, give or take, that she should spend as much time with her children as possible and—another careworn phrase—get her affairs in order? What about that? Is that what she wanted?

She tried to remain positive, or appear positive, at least. Everyone commented on that after she was gone, how deliberate she was as she gave away her jewelry, her knitting wool, her clothes. She did not think ahead to her children's adult years—that they might want to keep some of these possessions. No, she had decided to give them away. It was what she wanted, she said. In other words, she got what she wanted.

And this was false and saying it did not make anyone feel any better as she lay dying, or after she had died. Because what she had wanted was to live. That is what she wanted and what everyone who loved her wanted. They wanted her to defy the odds and live.

PUNCHBAG

for the women of Afghanistan,
in particular

No one had told her she would be a punch bag, that there would be blows, that she would have to remain silent as the blows fell, that she would perish if she protested her arranged marriage, for example. The punch bag—her body—deflated with each blow, all truth suspended like particles, like snowfall, like atoms after the big bang, like gunfire, like bombs.

She was in free fall. The grass, the sea, the sharp rocks edging the sea; this was her fate. Yet her skin was supple, her tender spirit permeated with the scent of flowers, the sweetness in the air, the salty sea and the flight of birds returning from their migration.

THE TRICK

for all the sex slaves, may they soon be free

Mid-flight, the young pilot summoned her. He requires release, the flight attendant said. It was a male crew, no women workers onboard except for the whore.

She had been dozing on and off, sipping on pomegranate mango juice and looking out of the window at the piebald sky. The seats next to her were empty as was most of the first class cabin. This was deliberate. The airline was owned by a prince.

In coach, families with children, sheikhs, government officials. Kabul to Abu Dhabi, non-stop. They knew nothing of the whore although some suspected her purpose during the long flight. Why else would a woman in full burka be traveling alone?

The desire to be veiled still possessed and protected her, or so she thought. Images of the rock quarry surfaced: her father, brothers and uncle selecting the stone, some of it soft, some of it hard, like life they always said when she complained of her fate. Out of the stone they made small chiseled sculptures of famous men and others of lubricious women to be sold from under the tables in the market. These sculptures were wrapped in cloth, suffocated, like the living models who had inspired them.

Now she was in a harem and there was stability in this, she told herself. There was a television, a cook, servants. The room behind the cockpit had been built for her especially. Fruit, beverages, music, a private w.c., perfumes and potions.

GET TO WORK LADIES

She could never do better than 40-words-per-minute. She was all thumbs. Sitting on her hands to make them warm at the beginning of the class didn't help, not a bit. Her hands got numb, she was bored. The only thing to read was the letter schemata in front of the room and the nonsensical paragraphs in the manual.

The teacher was a man who ran a typing school and worked at the high school one day a week. All that day he taught typing to young women and then recruited the best for his typing pool.

He was young and handsome. He wore a suit. The young women fantasized about his life, his wife, his children, where he lived. That was more fun than typing nonsensical paragraphs.

Doing this right is important, they were told. It was preparation for the life ahead as mature, marriageable women with children who may, one day, decide to go back to work as a secretary.

ARE YOU JEWISH?

The way it is, I don't want to be Jewish. Why be Jewish? The day before the day before yesterday, all my ancestors were Jewish. What does that mean? It wasn't enough and it still isn't enough to say I'm Jewish. Everyone pays attention to you when you are Jewish. They either notice or they don't notice or pretend not to notice. If they notice, they may hate you or, alternatively, pretend to love you. Those Jews, all those things they have accomplished. What things? When? They were just people working, doing stuff. What does being Jewish have to do with it? Do we have bigger brains? Are we more disciplined, more understanding? Do we pray more than other people? Can I say I am Jewish if I don't pray?

Remember the time we got into the elevator with our Christmas tree and our German neighbor got in and asked:

"What are you doing with that tree?"

"We're taking it home. We're going to decorate it."

"But you're Jewish."

"Mister, did I ever tell you I was Jewish?"

"No, but..."

"No but what? I'm about as Jewish as you are whatever you are."

I knew it wouldn't last, my not wanting to be Jewish. Someone is always around to remind me that I am.

WHY IS IT NECESSARY TO
KEEP WHAT'S OLD?

I am so glad you came by, the woman said. Make yourself at home, consider it your home. *Mi casa, su casa*, she said. We had only talked on the telephone once, exchanged emails. Best not to get too friendly, the realtor had said. Let's close the sale.

We closed the sale.

Then the old house came down, my mother's house, a split-level ranch circa 1960s, the infrastructure crumbling as my mother aged. Memories. The dog's ashes scattered near the swimming pool where we all—including the dog— swam. The pile of logs for the fireplace, pachysandra and azalea, lovingly planted, all ripped up and tossed away. Not even mulched, tossed into the dumpster.

How did I know this? Well, I went to the house after the sale to have one last look and the bulldozers were already there, a port-a-san for the workers, two dumpsters, one already full. I had written an email to say: please don't tear down the dogwood tree. That was my favorite. I will move it myself, if necessary, bring it up to my daughter's house.

But they tore down the tree. Tears. I made a phone call. The woman was very kind and said, please come round any time. You will be welcome. *Mi casa, su casa*, she said.

No apologies. No apologies necessary, I thought. Well, of course, this/me was not her problem.

It was a new white house with floor to ceiling windows, wall hangings, potted trees, Noguchi lighting, two fireplaces, and an open-plan kitchen. A family of four lived there: two adults, two children. It was their new home, their new beginning. They had sculpted the landscape to their own specifications. The house had been reoriented, the garage on the north side, the pool eliminated entirely, a greens-ward. There was nothing more to say but thank you. Thank you for understanding and welcoming me into your home.

THE PARADOX OF TIME

At risk of going out on a narrative limb, I shall try to be philosophical about the upcoming birthday which I do not, repeat—DO NOT—want to celebrate and believe me I am trying to be joyous about it, and philosophical as I keep saying, and all you are doing is insisting that I have a party, thank goodness at least it would not be a surprise as you are asking my permission. Thank you for asking my PERMISSION. *CON SU PERMISSO* I THINK WE SHOULD HAVE A PARTY TO COMMEMORATE YOUR BIG BIRTHDAY. *Con su permiso?* Commemorate? This sounds like a commemorative ceremony at Arlington National Cemetery. Is this ex post facto con *su permisso*? Have you already made arrangements at a restaurant of your choice, or found someone to cater the party in our home? What do you mean by CON SU PERMISSO when you have already started arranging a party? And you want me to make a list? I do not want to make a list. I do not want to have a party, *finito*. Do you not feel the paradox of time as described by Aristotle or was it Plato? Time goes, time stays, ah no, "time stays and we go," according to the poet Henry Austin Dobson (1804-1891). A party, therefore, will only create confusion.

A DEATH IN THE FAMILY

Sometimes she wakes up thinking about her grandmother's grave. She was worked to death at the age of 50. The killing had started long before when she was caught by the officers on the way home from work and forced—at gunpoint—to get down on her hands and knees to "wash" cobblestones. She had gone to school with some of them, loved one or two. Now they laughed. They smoked. They made ribald jokes about her breasts, her legs, her buttocks. They wanted to fuck her.

She was late and her family was worried. She finally arrived and told the story about the cobblestones, the onlookers, former friends and classmates, her humiliation and terror. Then came all the rest, which is history, but it is not the only history:

Two brothers are on a beach kicking around a ball, an older brother looking after a younger brother. The ball slips into the water and drifts away. Whose fault is it? No one's. But the older brother shoves his kid brother to the ground and starts kicking his head. And he kicks it and he kicks it and he kicks it until his kid brother is nearly dead. Then he stops and calls for help. And he never admits what he has done. But we all know what he has done.

BREAKING CHOCOLATE

The first time I thought of my brother after he had died was when I bought a bar of chocolate. It was dark Swiss chocolate. I took it with me everywhere and ate it slowly, one piece at a time, carefully broken along the seams. And when I finished one bar, I bought another, and then another.

Six months after his death I was on a double chair lift in Vermont with my boyfriend. The chocolate bar was in the inside pocket of my parka, but it was too cold for me to take off my mittens to retrieve it. When we got off the lift, before heading down the slope, I took it out. It was so cold, I couldn't break it, and this impotence made me incredibly sad. My brother would have broken it easily. I didn't want to cry in front of my boyfriend; I didn't think he would understand or care. And I was right. We ended our relationship after that trip because of our incompatibilities— emotion vs. restraint, mostly. "I can't stand your moods," he would say to me. To which my reply was always, "And I can't stand that you never have moods."

My brother was a strong man with thick powerful hands. He had figured out how to break chocolate with his thick hands even on the coldest days. I always knew that when I was with him the chocolate was guaranteed; it was mine.

BOYS AND GIRL

I was an anxious child who disliked being told what to do. I had to control my decisions and movements as best I could given my age. In this way, I avoided conflict with adults.

I hung out mostly with boys. Girls were too boring and predictable. I did not care about my hair or clothes. I could hit a softball into the outfield and wasn't afraid to ride my bike down the hill.

I felt safe with my boy-friends until one died.

I was twelve that year and had not experienced death at all. Barry was the boy's name. He was dead, my mother announced to me one day. *And that will show you not to ride down that hill on your bike.*

He had skidded, fallen off his bike and smashed his head. Cracked it right through, his brains gushing out on the pavement. Could my mother have been more graphic? *He was dead on arrival at the hospital. He will never pitch a ball again.*

Barry. I missed him before my mother stopped talking. Looking back now, I think he was the first boy I ever loved.

AN EMAIL FROM A FORMER FRIEND

I received an email from a former friend. The email consisted of a greeting, some recent news of successful accomplishments, and a planned business trip to the city. Despite the success of accomplishments, my former friend needed a place to stay.

The city where I live is expensive and daunting. My former friend had never traveled here on her own before. In fact, the last time she was here, she was with a boyfriend she had hoped and intended to marry, but unbeknownst to her, he had moved on—to someone else—and though he had paid for her trip, he had not told her that he moved on because he needed her to carry $10,000 in cash through customs for him. And she had agreed. It wasn't an illegal smuggle, not at all. He had also carried $10,000 in cash—the limit was $20,000—he needed $20,000 for a project he was working on in the city—and he needed my former friend, who would soon be his former girlfriend—to help him get the money into the country.

So there was all that kerfuffle. We—my husband and I—were in the midst of a difficult move during this money-carrying visit, and I didn't have time to spend with my friend unless she helped me pack and plan, which she refused. At the very least, she told me at the time, she wanted to see the sights, go to a couple of exhibitions, that kind of thing. Which I could not do.

We did meet for a lunch at a diner near our new apartment and we talked and tried to catch up. We'd maintained our friendship long-distance for a long time but now it was being tested. It didn't help that her boyfriend of ten years was about to move on, that I had no time to warn her of what was obvious: he had used her to get money into the country. And I couldn't commiserate enough, she later told me, and was clearly on her boyfriend's side, had been all along, why hadn't I warned her, and so on.

And the boyfriend—now a former boyfriend—had, as predicted, moved on. As soon as they'd arrived back in Italy, in fact, he'd taken a trip to Morocco with his new love. I called my former friend to commiserate several times and she either rushed me off the phone or was very cold. What had I done? I had no idea. Eventually, I stopped calling.

And now this email. Was it a reconciliation? There were no apologies. I looked around the apartment—we had downsized, it was small—and I realized I didn't want her to stay. Not at all. And I told her so—politely, gently and honestly.

CHILDREN AND DOGS

I had taken a walk in the morning and saw a toddler pushing a toy stroller, her parents on either side. Her mom was trying to shoot a video of these first outdoor steps on her smart phone. I stopped to watch and the little girl-child smiled at me and I smiled at her. "Learning to drive?" I said to her parents. And they smiled. And then I smiled again.

From this joyous encounter came other joyous encounters, one after the other that day. If not children, dogs. A small dog low to the ground with short brown fur, a pointy nose and amber eyes. I particularly like dogs with amber eyes. I particularly like dogs with brown fur, though black dogs I like too. The small dog low to the ground likes to eat snails. They are everywhere in the park this time of year—in the grass, under the benches. They must be very delicious— dog escargot. The thought of a low-to-the-ground dog enjoying the snails makes me smile.

It is said that we have to remain humble in order to be happy, to enjoy the small things in life, to take life as it blooms and wallows. I genuflect to this notion as though I were in church.

LIE BY THE OPEN WINDOW

Lie by the open window. Breathe. Listen to the birds. Watch the sky.

There was a storm last night, lightening and thunder, a strong wind. But this morning the birds are searching for the crumbs you left on the window sill and flitting to and fro in a joyful symphony of sound and motion.

We must thank the Conquistadores for the masted ships that carried birds across the turbulent sea. They survived the voyage. And so did we.

NOMADS 3

The Love Songs of Gulls

BEACH MEMORY

The sand had never been so hot, the air so dry. It was windy, the waves were high. He was lying face up on the blanket, his hat pulled over his eyes. She was standing, restless, casting a shadow onto his torso. The smell of oil and salt and sea. Half past one. Her thoughts sputtered and she said, "Let's swim." She reached for his arm and pulled it up. "Get up," she said. He laughed and pulled her down. His hat blew off. "Shit," he said as he drew her into his chest. The future opened: their love would fade. It was already half-buried in the dune.

INCUBATOR BABY

Even a baby has a story. She had been taken down for x-rays and was wrapped up inside the incubator, a little hat on her head, a striped blanket covering her and oxygen pumping through a tube into her nose. Such a small little baby. There were two nurses with stethoscopes around their necks, one on each side of the incubator. A priest was standing next to them, and when the elevator arrived, everyone gave way for the procession: two nurses, the baby inside the incubator, the priest. "This baby gets right of way," I said. Where were her parents? How could they have let their baby out of their sight? Why did she need an x-ray? I began to cry, just a soft, whispering cry. Then everyone in the elevator fell silent. The priest raised his finger and pressed it against the glass near the baby's head. He said a blessing. "This baby needs to be blessed," the priest said. So we all blessed the baby.

CYCLADIC WOMEN

Even though they felt like dancing, they were not permitted to dance. They were not only posed in the workshop, they were posed at the well, at the communal table, in the marriage bed. After a while their crossed arms automatically assumed the correct position under their breasts, the right above the left, a natural corset. Their breasts were bare, their navels exposed above wrapped linen skirts. The fabric fell to their ankles. Their foreheads were shaved, exposing their aquiline faces to the sun. Their eyes drooped modestly.

HE WAS EATING A GOAT'S NECK

It was very dark and I couldn't see the room in its entirety. A man was sitting at a table with a tankard in front of him. It could have been cider or beer. There was no wine in this establishment, a crude way-station on the way north. Horses were tethered at the back, on the side, and at the front. The roof sloped onto a decrepit drain, water dripping incessantly onto the stoop.

It had been a cold autumn. I was traveling on my own dressed as a man, escaping from the man I was supposed to marry; a dowry had been raised and presented.

I paid my two pence, dragged myself up the stairs, stashed my belongings, and returned to the main room for vittles. I asked what the man was eating and said I would have the same, tankard and all. But when it arrived, the odor was overwhelming. A goat's neck filled with nourishing marrow, the proprietor said. Would you have some potatoes? I asked. It was all I could stomach.

MR. VENDEM

A young girl lives in the woods far away from a construction site. The site has not always been there; it's new. Say an oil company has arrived, or gold diggers from Alaska, or diamond miners from South Africa. Say a pipeline is going to be built without regard for the villages or people in its path.

It's a warm sunny summer day and the child has been instructed by her mother to go to the store . All she wants to do is to return home quickly to play with her friends.

She's walking along at a brisk pace through the woods onto the dirt road when she hears machinery. Further along, she can see mechanical shovels and bull dozers. Further still, there is large sandy pit where the road used to be. She stops.

She walks to her left and then to her right searching for a path around the pit. She steps over rusty pipes and granite rocks. A man calls a warning to her. Get away, he says. The road is closed.

She sits down on the hard rocky ground. At least it's dry, she thinks to herself, grateful for once that there has not been a lot of rain. Then she moves closer to the pit and dangles her thin legs and bare feet over the edge. Finally, a big burly dark-skinned man wearing a bright red hard hat comes over to her. He asks her gently if she'd like some help? She explains that she is supposed to walk to the village to order supplies.

The man lifts her up and carries her to the other side of the pit. He's Mr. Vendem he tells her, better known as her Knight in Shining Armor. Mr. Vendem, she says. You are my Mr. Vendem.

And from then on, the young girl dreamt about him and hoped one day to marry him.

I WISH TO SAY

I wish to say that today is William Shakespeare's birthday. I am married to his mind in so many ways. As a compass turns, I turn with his every mood. If I am wrong, please correct me. Oh, no, I am not wrong, then let me continue before it is too late. And if I overstay my visit, feel free to remove me. I cannot alter my devotion or bend to anyone else's desires. It is Shakespeare I love. His worth is known to me and I will not damage his esteem of me. As for time's rosy lips that take me to the pinnacle of life, the very doom of existence shall sickle me. Oh, no, let me continue to write forever more in Shakespeare's presence with his every breath enlivening me.

A THRILLING AFTERNOON
WITH A GORILLA

I would like to report my afternoon at the zoo which began Friday last at approximately 11 a.m. I entered at the south gate and proceeded immediately to the "Congo Enclosure." I am happy to report that the guerrillas, as opposed to the gorillas, were in retreat. This was not planned or scheduled *per se*, but I had it in mind that it would be my first port of call, so to speak. On the way I passed one skinny tiger and two leopards. All three were pacing restlessly in their habitats. The four full-grown gorillas, on the other hand, were serene. Two of them were sleeping, one was searching for scraps of kale the keepers had provided, and a very large male came right up to the glass barrier. Was this normal? What would happen if the barrier broke? Of course it was enchanting to be so close to this wonderful creature. And he probably felt the same, don't you think? Because we are also enchanting creatures, are we not? We humans, I mean.

We "communicated" for several minutes eye to eye, pointed finger to pointed finger. The crowd around me was sweating. There was a strong smell, not of the gorillas, but of the humans gawking at the gorillas—myself included. The air was tropical, dense and unventilated. I thought I might faint, and when I came to, I had an epiphany: we were all imprisoned in this habitat together. The glass barrier was an illusion. Inside, outside, it made no difference. We had done this to the gorillas and to ourselves.

AND THIS IS MY ROAD

And this is my road. And this is my undulating road. And these are the turning leaves. And this is the unbroken road. And up ahead is the fork in the road. And this is the white line that looks like a skunk's back. The horizon. The clouds. The mountain, all this is mine. I can see it all from the road as I walk on the road. This is the road I have taken. And this is the road I have not taken. And this is the bend in the road. Beyond the trees are houses and people inside their houses and on their porches, a child on a tire swing, another playing ball. Beyond the trees and houses is a pond and a farm. Chickens, rabbits and pigs, vegetables, bats and mice, a family of bears, toads in the pond, chipmunks, a dog, a cat. And this is my road, my beautiful undulating road.

LEARNING TO DRIVE

My longing to drive was like a constant fever. My father let me take the wheel on a country dirt road and, later, in a parking lot. I was only fifteen but tall enough to look older. I could see over the wheel which helped. I wasn't afraid. I couldn't believe my luck. I wanted to drive all across the country and never stop. One day, I told my dad to get out of the car so I could see what it felt like to drive alone. He agreed and I took off, out of the parking lot, back onto the dirt road which led to the parkway, left signal on and off I went. He called the cops and they chased me for about ten miles. I wasn't going fast, only about 50 mph or so, but they didn't want to startle me into an accident. I was so self-assured, never for a minute did I think I'd have an accident. They gave me a stern warning and started laughing. They thought it was the funniest damn thing that a fifteen-year-old in pigtails had stolen her father's car. Little did they know what it meant to me.

ALEXI'S JOURNEY ACROSS
UNKNOWN CONTINENTS

Alexi has arrived in the city on horseback after many years of travel. He has long thick black hair and his body is lithe and strong. He is barefoot, nude from the waist up, sun-streaked, and hungry.

The year is 1510 BCE, the city is Alexandria. And though he has followed the stars, he does not know where he is. Perhaps at the edge of the world?

He follows the aroma of baking bread into a shop and holds out his hand like the beggars he has seen on the streets as he entered the city. They were either sitting cross-legged or sitting on their haunches. They reminded him of the animals in the forest. Some were moving among the crowds, their begging cups jangling with coins.

A young woman in the bakery stopped what she was doing and went to speak to her mistress in the back of the shop. *There is a man*, she said. The mistress came out to look at him. Alexi smiled.

It didn't take long for a crowd to gather. This man, was he a spy or simply a wanderer in search of destiny? Where were his clothes? Where had he come from? If they allowed him to remain in the city, what would become of him? What would become of them if he returned to his kingdom and reported their wealth and well-being?

Alexandria was a model of enlightenment in those days. Rather than kill the traveler or imprison him, they put him to work in the bakery and gave him a storage room to sleep in. Eventually, he found a woman, had children, grew old, and died peacefully in his adopted city.

HOW THE CONVERSATION ENDED

A man and a woman are spending the afternoon together at a museum. It will be their last afternoon together for a while, or perhaps forever.

They meet at 3:30 p.m. They are always both on time and this last time is no different. They check their bags, pay, and enter. The man is wearing a colorful short-sleeved shirt. The woman is wearing long earrings. They do not comment on their attire, their appearance, or anything about their personal attachment; they are focused on the art.

Some of the portraits are very large, some are smaller, all are of noble men and women in the 17th century Dutch court. Most are wearing starched millstone collars, an emblem of prosperity.

"How uncomfortable they must have been," she says.

He does not agree or disagree. He walks away with his hand to his chin, or both hands behind his back.

They stroll onto the avenue to look for a café. It is the first warm day of summer.

"I do not want to walk far," she says.

She orders a latté, he orders a glass of wine.

"Don't worry, I'm not going to disappear," he says.

"But you have sold everything," she reminds him. "Even your television set."

EATING PRUNES

She had just arrived from Monaco and was on the terrace eating prunes. He was behind the wicker settee sitting cross-legged, meditating, oblivious to her arrival. She had been preparing a speech during the journey home and had even written it out several times. A declamation as much as a declaration, she thought to herself. She would ask him to listen without interrupting her.

How poetic it was, her longing for him. How persistent and inexplicable. He was not worthy. He was not even there in the corporeal sense.

You can't do this to me, she began. She had the urge to touch the top of his head. It took her only a few moments to realize the futility of the gesture and she withdrew her hand before it touched him.

This wasn't love, it was a fantasy. He was a canvas on which she had painted her life.

A LOVE STORY ABOUT A BOW

for mf

First, the musician chooses the not yet endangered Brazilian permambuco wood. He has rejected the snake wood. He has rejected the synthetic carbon. He holds the permambuco vertically and strokes it north to south. He holds it to his ear. He says to the bow maker: This is my wood. I can hear the rainforest in this wood.

Then the bowmaker says: I have a horse's tail from Siberia. I will make you this bow.

And the musician says: I have to like the bow and the bow has to like my cello, and when I place the bow upon my cello, the cello and the bow have to sing to me.

MY LITTLE ORPHAN BOY

Don't be angry if he doesn't listen to you, they said. He won't listen to you. Reduce your breathing to 4-6 breaths per minute. Chant, if necessary: *My little orphan boy. My little orphan boy.* You have adopted this child at two. And there have been rumors from whence he came. Rumors, not facts. One can only imagine.

After a while—and one does not know how long—there will be adjustments, there will be understanding. Eventually, there will be love.

AFTER THE WEDDING

Say, for example, we are attached to someone of the same gender and then this person marries someone of the opposite gender. We assume it has nothing to do with us, it is for appearance only, for the sake of career advancement, or the reputation of a family that cares about such things. There has been no explanation, only an announcement, and then an invitation to the wedding itself.

How are we to dress? Will we be able to smile? To dance? To offer our hand in congratulation to the fortunate bride, to hug our special friend and whisper into his ear: I shall miss you.

HE'S SO SWEET

for Dolly Parton

He's so lovely, he's so sweet, he's my honey, he's so neat.
He's my angel, he's my love, he's my lover, he's my dove.

He's so lovely, he's so sweet, he's my honey, he's so neat.
He's my he-man, he's my love, he's so special, he's my
dove.

He's so lovely, he's so sweet, he's my honey, he's my love,
he went roaming in the cove.

I'm so bitter, I'm so blue, I can't figure out what's true.

ARE YOU SEXY?

What I need is an answer, he said. Are you sexy?

How should I know, I said.

I didn't like his voice. It was hoarse, demanding, over-confident.

If you aren't sexy, why should I be interested?

I don't care if you are interested or not, I said. I am doing this for the money. College loans. If you like my picture and my profile, I'll come over. I can't stay on the phone much longer.

10 p.m., he said. Then he gave me the address. Take a cab, he said. Put it on my bill.

It was in an upscale neighborhood north of Georgetown. The lights were on in every room. Secret Service at the door, two men, straight as poles, ear pieces, gray suits, dark blue ties.

They opened the door without even one question. No credentials. No proof of anything. They didn't search my bag. I could have been anyone, an assassin even.

They'd had instructions, he told me. Let her in. She's a friend of my daughter's.

LOL, I was the same age as his daughter!

You mean to tell me the Secret Service didn't know he was alone? That his daughter and his wife were traveling somewhere? Even I knew that. I watch the news.

It was just ordinary, boring sex. I don't know why he bothered, why he took the risk.

WHY DOES HE ALWAYS WEAR BLACK?

A black turtle neck, black slacks, this is his uniform, day in and day out. In summer it's black T-shirts and black linen pants, always black, drowning in black. His house is bare of furniture, the fridge is empty. In the freezer, a few items: not food, but toys. Scrabble tiles in a hand-crocheted sack (stiff from cold), a plastic dildo (stiffer from cold). She asks if he'd like to play. What? he asks. Both, she says.

In the living room there are choices: free-standing designer chairs (three of them) and a 1950's barely upholstered black sofa. She suggests they sit side by side. Are you ready to make love? she asks. Or would you rather place a letter on the board? There's no board, he says.

They walk to the window arm in arm. They are high up and the sunlight at this altitude is blinding. She leans into him. There is no resistance, neither is there any encouragement.

SEDUCED BY A FOUNTAIN PEN

They were at a party sitting around a low coffee table filled to overflowing with food. Their host was Armenian, a very good cook. And then there was the booze, everyone well lubricated, and the exotic music, a few people dancing. San Francisco. The 1990's. A mixed crowd.

He took out his fountain pen, unscrewed the top, and asked if she had a piece of paper. "Is that a real Montblanc?" She had never owned a Montblanc, had never known anyone who did. She handed him a small notebook she kept in her purse, spiral bound.

"There's a book I want to tell you about," he said. "I'll write down the title. While I'm doing that you can give me your phone number."

This wasn't a request. He didn't ask permission. He just took the number down as though it had always belonged to him. She watched the blue-black ink slide out of the nib, like blood exiting a vein.

A week later he invited her to dinner. He didn't care that she was married. And she didn't either, apparently, because she said yes. She told her husband and he was amused.

"But he didn't invite you," she said.

"It doesn't matter," he said.

So she went.

She didn't like the food or the pretentious waiter with his long list of specials. But the man—this man, this strange man—seemed to enjoy it all. Why had he invited her? Why had she accepted?

Then, at one point, during a lull in the conversation, she asked to borrow his Montblanc pen. With a flourish, she took out her spiral notebook and added a few items to her shopping list.

THE DIVINE SARAH

The most famous actress the world has ever known stepped into the vertical railroad at The Players Club in New York on November 10, 1890. This was, and still is, a one-person elevator with red walls and a small gate that the passenger must close herself from inside.

Why didn't The Divine Sarah walk up the stairs? It was a beautiful carpeted staircase leading from the ground level to the fourth floor. But her manager had said, "You are tired my dear, take the lift." He was British so the word he used to describe the new contraption was "lift."

The Divine Sarah stepped into the lift and was instructed by the concierge: "Close the gate, Madam," and he demonstrated with a theatrical gesture in her honor.

But the gate was not entirely closed. The elevator moved and then it stopped between floors. The Divine Sarah began to swear and shout. "This is a good opportunity to practice your English," her manager said.

The Fire Department was called. They arrived *post haste*, but when they discovered the object of the rescue, they became oddly paralyzed. It was almost an hour before The Divine Sarah was released from captivity. Feeling only slightly woozy, she decided to feint a faint.

The next day, the incident was reported in the newspapers: "I was in utter despair, weeping bitter tears that stained my cheeks," The Divine Sarah said.

And everyone believed her.

THE EMPRESS DOWAGER CIXI

Her body is her minaret, her throne a bird, the chamber pot a gilded scented lemon. Visitors to the court are not permitted to sit, they must stand. All the doors are open to the manicured gardens, etched in stone and hibiscus. A shrine with baby shoes, baby hair, discarded buttons and zippers, emblems of Mongolian ancestry and imperial prowess. Her feet, unlike the Mandarin ladies in her court, remain unbound.

WHO DO YOU THINK YOU ARE?

in memory of Malick Sidibé

A woman with a flower. *La femme avec un fleur.* I prefer it in French, he says. *La femme avec un fleur.*

At each session, he asks, "Who do you think you are?" He likes to see his models dance. When we dance we express who we really are. "What is real about you?" he asks.

Here, for example, is a man who drives a taxi, a taximan. *Taximan avec voiture.* He stands next to his vehicle, an extension of his very self.

The stars belong to you, he says of his models, especially when we are young, especially when we dance.

THE MAN WHO BLEW ME A KISS

I was in a cafe in Vila Nova De Milfontes. It faced the sea and it was dusk. And though the sky is beautiful everywhere, it was particularly golden that warm summer evening in Portugal. I was there on holiday and I was alone, looking for holiday love.

The cafe was crowded. In fact, there was only one seat available at a table near the floor to ceiling glass window. A man was sitting there. I couldn't see his face but from the back he looked handsome. He sat straight, had a full head of hair and a long torso. I like tall men.

I am not usually a bold woman but on holiday I try to reinvent myself. No one I know from home is there to observe or criticize. I can be a vamp if I wish. I can dress any way I please. I let the circumstance and my mood guide me.

I approached the table and sucked in my breath. "May I share the table with you, Senhor?"

I spoke in English; I cannot speak Spanish or Portuguese though I should know Spanish by now as I am from New York. But I don't.

The man turned his head towards me—I was now standing on his left—and gestured for me to sit down. He was old. An old man with a young, upright body. I had not expected this and, needless to say, I was disappointed. I called for the waiter and put the novel I was reading on the table. The man watched me intently. He had deep-set eyes, a scraggly beard, and weatherworn skin. A fisherman perhaps? His small straw hat was turned upside down in front of him. His clothes were soiled and he looked like a beggar.

I was absorbed in my novel when the waiter returned with my coffee. The old man was mute and I remained mute in his presence. I very much wanted to be sitting at another table but I also did not want to be rude. So I continued reading and sipping on my coffee. The man had nothing in front of him but his upturned straw hat.

Several minutes passed. I looked up and he was still watching me intently. The waiter came over and put his hand on the man's shoulder. "Pai," I heard him say. That much I could understand. This man was his father. Were they talking about me? "Are you talking about me?" I asked the waiter. And I pointed to myself. Oh, it was a great misunderstanding. The old man reached over the table with one of his rough hands. And with the other he blew me a kiss. He blew me a kiss! I couldn't believe it. Even worse, everyone in the cafe was looking at me and laughing.

THE WEEK THE CAT DISAPPEARED

That feral, feisty cat, so loved.

When should we stop calling for her? When should we stop looking for her? When should be put away her food, dump her litter, toss her bed? When should we sweep up all the cat hair, get out the vacuum cleaner? When should we take down the signs?

What if we find her body on the road, or in the woods, or splayed on the electric fence? What if she suffered? What if she called out to us with her insistent meow?

When will we stop imagining her appearance on the stoop at supper time or first thing in the morning? When will her presence become a memory? When will we begin to talk about her in the past tense? When will our grief subside? When will we be able to post a eulogy on Facebook? When should we get a new kitten?

WISH YOU WERE HERE

What stirs me is the small stories they tell, the careful handwriting and the salutations: dearest, dear, with love, with everlasting affection, and so on. I have never received or sent any postcards like those I collect, nor am I nostalgic for any trips I have taken to faraway places such as Niagara Falls, for example. There was no one in my life at the time I wanted to write to about my trip. I just went, enjoyed the falls, talked to one or two people, and came home.

So it confounds me that people would document their trips with a postcard to friends and relatives. Why bother when they will only end up at a thrift store or in my house?

WINTER MEMORY

The school year began: new crayons, notebook, lunchbox, pens and pencils, a pencil case, new shoes (we'd grown, we were spurting), hems down on our dresses, new dresses, a new winter jacket.

It was just weeks before the first puff of cold air, gloves and snowflakes, bells on our shoelaces. We didn't own dolls, or maybe just one or two decoratively placed on a shelf above our beds. We read comics, watched "The Lone Ranger," ice skated once or twice a week. It was cold, biting. We skated anyway.

I remember the sleds, too, wooden with metal blades, the snow packed thick enough to create a cushion, snow piled on top of cars up to the back window, snow days without a mayor's equivocation—should we or shouldn't we shut the schools?

COWS

I walked down the cow path early in the morning. It had rained and the smell of hay and dung was sweet. There were butterflies and bluebells to keep me company, otherwise I was alone for a while. I heard their bells approaching and picked up my pace. I didn't not want to walk with the cows that morning, or next to them, or behind them. I had just released them into the pasture and was headed home for breakfast. I would see them again at day's end and spend more time.

They followed me. They had started doing this of late, it was instinctual. No matter how busy I was, I needed them— their hot breath, their sweet eyes—and, miraculously, they sensed my need.

I walked slowly as they approached and turned. They were of varying colors: brown and black and white. They were large long-haired cows with a rolling gait. Some of them had just calved, others were still pregnant. The sight of them made me smile.

They ambled gently to the edge of the path and stopped. They stood in a line, one after the other waiting for my command to enter the path.

What Did You Expect Would Happen?

FEELING THE KILL

It was five years after the end of the Civil War and two of the neighbors had been Union soldiers. They had wives and children, animals, shelter, food and a community of neighbors helping one another to return to. In all this, they were blessed.

On that hot July morning one of the black barn cats had escaped onto the road and the rabbits were eating their breakfast with gusto like prisoners downing their last supper and the rooster was hooting incessantly and the ducks were in and out of the pond and the dogs were chasing them. The orchard was nearly complete with a grape arbor and fruit trees, a blueberry patch and a clover field for the bees.

The kill station had been set up at the far end of the property and the rabbits, one by one, were brought there for slaughter. Six neighbors were there to to help and they prayed and blessed the rabbits and thanked them.

But that night at dinner, the neighbors gathered to partake of their bounty, the rabbits roasting on an open fire, something was different. One of the soldiers—his name was Jack—put down his fork. He looked at the meat and saw before him the torn, singed flesh of his fallen comrades and he smelled the rotting flesh of their wounds.

I CAN'T BELIEVE THEY'RE GONE

Every so often, usually when I am cooking or washing the dishes or making the beds or cleaning the bathroom—and why then, just at those moments, I have no idea—I think about the people I've known and loved who are gone.

Oh, I think, as I am watering the plants, I can't call my mother today, she's not there. Or my friend, Dan. An illness took him too young. I can still hear him playing the jazz piano—by ear, he couldn't read notes. I want to call to tell him how much I love Bill Evans these days, but he's gone, and I can't call him. (And Bill Evans is gone, too.)

And what about my brother who is still very much alive but won't talk to me. What about him? And should he even be included in this story?

And what about me? Will there be someone—anyone— somewhere in the future who will think about calling me and then remember that I am gone?

MY VOICES

for s

I lie awake in the cool darkness and pray that they have not followed me here. I am secluded in this house, all doors and windows locked, a knife under my pillow. But if they find me, I will surrender.

My voices tell me they will arrive by boat. They will be well armed; my knife will be useless. I will not recognize them and I will not understand their language. My cat will flee into the rafters.

I have not eaten for several days. Messages arrive as I sleep and I have been afraid to drive to town for provisions. They have poisoned the water. Once it is dark, I walk through the high grass to the lake and fill a small bucket with water. I drain it, then boil it. So far I have not been sick. But I am hungry.

What will they do to me if I am captured? If I could imagine my captivity I might feel safe again. Imagination is anticipation, is it not? They will arrive, they will shackle me and they will take me away. I will spend the remainder of my life in the bosom of my tormentors.

NON FINITO

inspired by Colm Tóibín's "Brooklyn"

Homeward bound. Just because she is returning does not mean the story is finished or that the canvas of her life is complete. There are more years ahead, for which she is grateful. She is still young. She has remained healthy despite her ordeal.

She did not get sick on the return voyage. Outbound, she had filled a bucket with vomit. The solution was obvious: do not eat.

It wasn't only the roiling ship, it was her fright and her sorrow. Her mother and sister had waved to her from the dock. This parting was too hard to bear.

The man who waited for her in San Francisco shook her hand, picked up her suitcase and steered her, his hand on the small of her back, to his car. There was a driver. It appeared that he had been telling the truth in his letters: he was rich.

Her uncle had arranged this marriage. It was forbidden in America which meant nothing. If she was asked, her answer—in halting English—would be, "Yes this is my husband." She had memorized his name, his origins, his occupation, where they would live.

It took her a year to find the courage to escape. In truth, the man was kind enough, at times. But as soon as she saw him, she knew she would not stay.

NOTICE OF A DATA BREACH

We would like to make sure you have the facts about what happened and what steps we are taking to protect your savings. Shortly before Christmas—and we apologize for taking such a long time to inform you—we noticed that our data had been stolen. All our data, including yours. Our CEO has already re-settled in Greenland with his cat and, for the moment, is unreachable. In fact, everyone on our team is unreachable. We no longer have an email address or an 800 telephone number. We have closed down our offices.

We would like to reassure you that this is an ongoing international investigation. When it is complete someone—and we cannot say who this will be—will contact you.

MEMORABILIA

There were secret sanctuaries. They realized this as soon as they entered the house after her death. Boxes inside boxes, folders inside folders, a hidden panel in the guest room closet. They pried it open easily with a fork. "Not that hidden," the lawyer said. The locks had been changed. They had not been allowed onto the premises unless the lawyer was present. And that was a shock, one among many.

The will was in dispute. Various paintings had been designated for this person or that. Furniture to Goodwill. Books to the local library. The piano to a favorite grandchild. There were two children—sons—and each of them had two children. And they were already arguing when, suddenly, a half-sister appeared. Due diligence, she had been found.

She had been living in Rio for three decades. This was the disappeared child, the abandoned child, the one who had been given away. Pregnancy, adoption and suddenly this heir appears, the lawyer explained. "Stand down. All will be resolved during probate. You cannot claim anything," she told the two sons.

These two brothers were as different as pie and cheese. One was mostly interested in old photographs, the other in the valuable paintings, furniture and a crystal collection.

Both of them hated their mother; she had a dry heart. After their father died, if they saw her once a year, it was too much. Neither did they enjoy one another's company. And now they were at each other's throat, an accurate description of inheritance disputes. Not a cliché at all.

The missing sibling arrived from Rio and arranged to meet the lawyer at the house, which had become a "premise," the premise being that the lawyer would have to decide everything. She unlocked the door: everything but the kitchen had been stripped bare.

"Now my work really begins," said the lawyer, and she called the cops. They arrived and took a report. But before any investigation began, the two brothers met with the lawyer. They had divided the spoils between them and had no interest in meeting their sister. They refused to return anything to the house.

"Breaking and entering," the lawyer said. "To what end?"

"Memorabilia," the brothers explained, almost as one person.

But of course that was not the end of the story, it never is. A court date was set, the discarded sister returned from Rio. This was more than three years later. In the meantime, the house had been sold, the proceeds placed in escrow. It just about covered the lawyer's bills.

FRIEND INVENTORY IN THE AGE
OF ELECTRONIC MEDIA

It's my birthday week and I am taking an inventory of my friends. This is probably not a good idea but I can't resist. I've done it before, years ago, when I was "transitioning" as they say—they meaning the me-psychology pundits—from one job to another, from one country to another, and from one steady relationship to no relationship at all. The list was long; I left many friends behind on another continent. And I wept as I wrote the list. We stayed in touch for a while, these friends and I, via phone calls, long letters and the occasional visit.

This time no transitioning, just the usual self-pity during my birthday week. Who loves me? Who will remember me? Will my snail mailbox be empty? Will my email mailbox be filled with junk and trash or will there be some happy bappy electronic greeting cards? Will I get any phone calls or texts or Facebook messages? Will anyone offer to take me out to lunch? Why do I miss my long-dead lover? What kind of inventory is this?

I have already decided what I am going to say on my Facebook page: Thanks for your happy birthday greetings. Please call me. I miss your voice. If you are nearby, let's get together.

ARE YOU A GRANNY?

Sometimes strangers ask me if I am a granny. I'm not a granny but even if I were a granny I wouldn't want to be a granny. Grannies are old. I am not old. Grannies are retired. I am not retired. Grannies are not interested or curious or fit. I am interested and curious and fit. Also, I have a name. Whoever you are, please call me by my name. That name has been with me all my life, and although it is not what I might have chosen, there's worn callous around it, like a rock.

Look at me stranger. Look into my eyes. Ask me questions about my life and what I'm doing right now. Never mind how old you think I am or where I should be in my life based on how old you think I am or what my relationship is to the person who is introducing us. Don't get glazed over with expectation when you see my silver hair which, by the way, is fashionably silver and pretty damn gorgeous if I do say so myself. Get to know me. Don't assume anything.

AN ARGUMENT IN FAVOR
OF BEHEADINGS

Beheading with a sword goes back a long way in history because, like hanging, it was both cheap and practical and, let's be frank, a sword was always readily available. For these very reasons—the availability, the cheapness, the practicality—we should approve of this form of execution and write it into law once again. I speak for my constituents in this matter. Many have petitioned me in recent months. Simple, clean, fast, no apparatus required other than the sword, available in every household, as I have said.

Some more historical context: Beheading continued in Britain up to 1747 and was the standard method in Norway (abolished 1905), Sweden (abolished 1903) and Denmark (abolished 1892). It was used for some classes of prisoners in France until the introduction of the guillotine in 1792 and in Germany up to 1938. We all know what happened after that: chimneys.

As for the Chinese, they replaced beheadings with shooting—also fast, but the equipment required is both expensive and difficult for some to handle. Considering the volume of guns in the United States, however, shooting might still be preferable to beheading in some states.

Madam Chairwoman, I yield my time.

AN ADVERTORIAL

I don't recall what final insanity drove me away or what season it was when I began to watch television all day long, the sound and images like wallpaper in my room. It was one room, my only room, all my distilled possessions stuffed into three drawers, one small closet, and a desk. I piled my remaining books on the desk and the rickety bedside table. I didn't have trouble giving things away. I like to give things away and see the joy on someone's face as they receive an unexpected gift, a piece of jewelry, for example. I know what my friends like, what they covet. I had no desire for anything sparkly or joyous. I had to find joy elsewhere, in the giving itself, in the sunrise. I was grateful I could sleep through the night. My cousin had taught me how to sing so I began to sing pop songs as they played on the radio. The air whistled through my teeth. My boots were warm. I was grateful for that, too. The television worked, the cable was free. I was glued to Dr. Oz who had advice for me about staying healthy, slim and positive. I couldn't figure out where the advice ended and the ads began. Maybe they were one and the same. One morning I woke up crying, I remember that now. At least you are feeling something, I said to myself. I was relieved and, once again, grateful, that I could still feel something. I think Dr. Oz would have been pleased with the result of his advertorial. I've always been open to whatever experts tell me. That's what landed me here in this room near the railroad tracks of this unforgiving city.

OUR PARALLEL UNIVERSE

for Paris

When you walk towards me like someone you haven't seen for decades. When you take off your coat and hang it on the chair, apologetic for falling out of touch, your cheeks rosy from your latest excursion abroad. Stories about airport lounges and missed connections, security at every portal, a bag of rice. You had wanted to marry, it was arranged, then broken. A mishap, you explained. A new sweater and shoes from a Paris boutique, euros bulging out of your purse like lava oozing from an exploded volcano, the disarray and chaos expressing itself in spite of itself.

I could not understand your insouciance. The road was dividing like a wave, a shattering outside the cafe, screams, the chop of helicopters. Blood everywhere. I could not see our future and I was sorry about yours and what you had done to it out of spite. I wished otherwise.

The sky was falling. Shards. Particles of bone, a bent bicycle, its wheel spinning. Your body was soft against mine. I said: *It's alright, it will be over soon.*

And it was.

THE USES AND ABUSES OF HELICOPTERS

After the briefing, the pilots talked in low tones. They had orders to scan the city for anti-aircraft weapons. This was possible because helicopters fly at low altitude, but it is also dangerous. Laser lights off the high buildings, sharp as knives. Tripwires. Propellants.

That night, the New York Mets had won the pennant and the Empire State was lit up. As soon as they were air-bound, the lights began to flash: blue, orange, blue orange. Insider information, this was their signal to attack.

They retreated without injury to themselves. And the next time they went up—this time to check the weather and any movement that remained in the destroyed city—they were escorted by fighter planes and clouds.

WAR DOGS

Afterwards, when we were lying naked in the field we opened our eyes and they were there—the dogs we had trained—exploded like burst melons, all ten of them. We'd been told not to give them names. They were Canine #1, Canine #2, and so on. We were to trade off—a different dog, a different handler—every day. Our instructions were: no favorites, no attachment, no hesitation. Movement and force without sentiment, that was battlefield mantra, or some would say hypocrisy, or some would say delusion, a trick. None of the tricks worked. The dogs licked us, nuzzled us when we praised them, and they were loyal. In their last battle they had returned to save us.

MONGRELS

The mongrels have been lined up against the wall. Abject and hungry they will either be put to work or shot. Woe to those who hesitate or faint into the ditch by the side of the road. One soldier spits, then another. Townspeople—former friends—line the road behind the barricade. Some are carrying flags, others shout slogans. Children are excited by the spectacle.

An accordion player wearing cardboard shoes plays a famous tune. An old man dances as the shop fronts cast a shadow on his grinning face. One has seen him before and wondered of his origins: mongrel or pure?

Soft windy rain falls on the street and buries it in remorse.

OVENS

They are not for baking cakes or cupcakes or chickens. They do not have racks. The heat never cools. The smoke coming out of the chimney does not smell like vanilla.

REFUGEE

Because I was tired, I took a walk to get some air. I walked into the park. It was windy. Most of the blossoms were finished, wilted or scattering in the wind. I felt lonely. I had travelled a great distance, across two oceans, across time zones. No one picked me up at the airport. There was no one to ask: How was your journey? Are you hungry? I was suddenly unable to tell time. All that I had managed so far in my life was useless to me. Remembering what they had done to my wife was the hardest. Now I was angry. Angry and alone. I felt chilled. I wanted to go home. I sat on a bench and watched a barge on the river. The water was brown, the barge was black, white and red. I was learning these words in English. Sometimes in class, I laughed with the others. But as soon as I laughed I also wanted to cry.

SEX SLAVE

for all the kidnapped girls

I am the last sex slave alive in the camp. It's almost two years later and I am grateful I have not been incinerated or died of starvation. I can hardly remember where I was before. The paths are lined with bodies, the barracks reek of excrement, sweat, spoiled food and anguish. My windows have curtains to keep out the sun and prying eyes. I spread my legs. What would you like I ask? What will give you pleasure? Sometimes they bring cake. Sometimes they bring chocolate. They allow me to bathe. They allow me to walk the perimeter of the camp. The soldier in the guard tower waves and smiles. Once, he brought me a flower. The one-eyed Commandant brings me lingerie and cooked chickens. You need sustenance he explains kindly. I don't have a schedule or an appointment book. I never know who will appear in my cottage or when. I recall, once upon a time, I was an artist.

And then when it is over and the camp is mostly quiet, I hear gunshots in the distance and then running and wild voices. And you are the first to arrive. You wrap me in blankets and take me to the field hospital. You cut my hair and examine me. Then you ask me to tell my story. I am telling you my story.

THE RE-ENACTMENT

Let's say it's early morning, cool and breezy, and the small green buds are beginning to open into figs and grapes in the arbor. The dog has been hunting and the cat is walking the parapet, slithering into danger, and you realize that for several months, maybe even years, you've played a similar role, grunting and moaning with something like desire, but more like pain—you're trying to define it—longing perhaps?

Sometimes our rational minds are out of control, wisdom suspended, all we have learned is forgotten. Our good sense, our conscience, our education, ceases to exist. We become meat.

Let's say it's an accident. Let's say there's forgiveness. Let's say the weather has turned. Let's say we're afraid. Let's say we follow orders.

Then one day, our muscles strengthen. We purchase armaments.

The cave opens. All the bones of our past are buried there.

SPECIAL POWERS

Once, not so very long ago, a magician's assistant told me she could see my aura. We were visiting her Dutch stone house deep in the countryside, and while my husband was interviewing her very famous magician husband for a magazine article, she took me and my five-year-old daughter to the barn to look at some paraphernalia stored in trunks. All the tricks of the trade were visible, she said, if only we chose to see them. She opened a trunk and took out a mirror, a saw, some hats, a stuffed rabbit. And, by-the-by, she said, I can see your aura. And though I knew that this, too, might be a trick, I was nearly incapacitated by this revelation. It held a power I could not resist. And the odd thing is that I cannot remember what color the aura was or what it signified. She just said she saw it and that was enough to frighten me. Maybe it was the look in her eyes; she had become a predator. I was her prey. It was like a spell and for an instant I felt faint. Then I came to and wanted to flee. I drew my daughter closer into my body, put my arm around her, held her tight, and said to the magician's assistant with the Russian name, "We'll be going now." I turned tail, literally, and walked my daughter briskly out of the barn. I opened the car door, snapped on our seat belts, revved the engine, and took off down the hard dirt driveway.

This was before the days of cell phones. I knew I'd have to return soon enough to pick up my husband. Why had he taken us along? He wanted us to have a day in the country, he had said, and magicians are, of course, fascinating people. So we went along.

I stopped at a diner and ordered some hot chocolate for my daughter and tea for me. Eventually, I calmed down. My daughter was calm, she seemed okay. I was not okay. I hadn't asked this woman to share her so-called special powers with me. Why did she presume to impose them on us?

We returned to the house and went into the parlor where the interview was taking place. The magician's assistant, who was also the magician's wife, was nowhere to be seen and that was fine with me. I told my husband that I wanted to leave, I wasn't well (a half-truth, a half-lie), and he'd have to complete the interview another time.

FIRE MEMORY

You'll be waiting for a happy ending to this story. That's why you are listening. The fire had started and there was a detour. We were on the way home after a placid weekend in the country with friends. The kids were in the back seat and they were hungry and tired. We were hungry and tired. The sky clouded over though it wasn't a cloudy day. No visibility. A cop with a flashlight a few yards ahead was barely visible. Detour, he shouted, and he pointed to his left.

There weren't many cars. We moved slowly onto a dirt road. Where are we going? my wife asked. The kids started crying. Kids are like dogs; they know. What were they sensing that we hadn't figured out?

We weren't driving away from the fire, we were driving into it.

Stupid cop, I said.

I lost sight of the car in front of us. Maybe it had turned and I hadn't noticed because, suddenly, we were alone on the road and the fields on either side were burning. The flames were weak and low to the ground. But what if the wind picked up? Suddenly I remembered everything I'd learned about fires when I was a volunteer forester. I remembered that if there were no trees and no wind, the fire would die out. Otherwise, we would.

THE WOMAN WITH THE
TUMOR IN HER CHEEK

As soon as she gets on the train she begins to talk. The talk becomes a whine, the whine becomes a harangue.

We've all seen her many times, seen her, and looked away. The tumor is real and it's getting bigger. It's somewhere between her right upper gum and cheek, as big as an orange or a tennis ball. Her dusty blonde hair is in a ponytail and she's thin, thin as an addict. Her clothes look clean, her hair looks clean. She doesn't smell.

So what if this tumor is real <u>and</u> she is an addict? What then? She's carrying a translucent plastic container for money. A few dollar bills, some coins. Most of us look away. We try to read. We tell ourselves: she's an addict, don't give her money. Offer her food, ask if she knows where to get help.

Some days, I want to take her by the shoulders and heave her out of the train. Or tell her to shut up. Once, I saw four young men do this to a ranting and raving lunatic. "No one wants to listen to this shit," one of them said. They grabbed him by his shoulders and threw him out of the train. Bravo, everyone shouted, and clapped.

The train moves too slowly between stops. I begin to listen to the story about the tumor, how it's getting bigger, it won't stop growing. How if she only had money a doctor at a famous hospital would operate. How does this make sense? How is it possible that this woman wouldn't be taken care of if she walked into an emergency room? It doesn't compute. "She's lying," I say to my neighbor who has closed his iPad and taken out his wallet.

THE GIRL IN THE MIRROR

after Picasso

Once upon a time a girl looked at herself in a magic mirror. She could see her present happy childhood, her not so long ago past, and her future.

In the present and the past were her parents, the most loving mother and father in all the world. In the future was a princely husband and three children of her own. As she was still young, and not yet mature enough to marry when she first began to use the magic mirror, she preferred contemplating the future rather than the present or the past. This was understandable. But then she reached maturity, married a princely man, and had three children of her own. Even so, she only looked into the magic mirror when it reflected the future. She did not need the mirror to teach her anything about her daily life, and so she avoided any troublesome reflections about her present. And as the past was past, she was not interested in it either even though memories of her idyllic childhood resided there.

Time passed and the past retreated further, the present became the past, and the future continued, for a while anyway, to stretch in front of the woman who was no longer young. Yet, as before, she did not concern herself with the past and all its consequences and discomforting thoughts. And as the past slipped away, she neglected her aging devoted parents and soon forgot them. Now when she looked into the magic mirror and saw the future, she was not pleased because her own children had forgotten her.

JEALOUSY NULLIFIED

In times of personal trouble and despair, I turn to the news. Immediately all resentment, fear and jealousy is nullified. I dream. I dream of a holiday in Canada. I dream of moving to Canada.

I arrive at mental clearings and speak only from my deepest pain. I do not hide my pain to spare my friends or family. I am a hamburger roasting on the grill charred black by forgetfulness. I have been left there while the party on the patio continues.

STORY OF REGRET
FOR VARIOUS OBJECTS

What we decided to do didn't seem so bad at the time. We stood in the living room and made lists: what to take, what to give away. It was a necessary departure, we said, and I suppose we were right, at the start anyway.

We culled, we distilled, we had a party. Someone brought balloons with the words: *Good-bye*. That didn't seem accurate. It wasn't good and it wasn't bye the bye. It was permanent, never to return. But we didn't know that at the time either.

We labeled the furniture and put the books and clothes on the bed. We told everyone to help themselves. There were discussions about this and that and then a frenzy. The greed surprised us. One or two people were embarrassed and said they had, perhaps, taken too much. They put one or two things back. We understood that it was hard to resist a giveaway, easy to forget that the giveaway was because of our getaway.

We should have done this more often, we said, ruefully. A clearing out, a reinvention. But the tears were rolling down our cheeks. Rueful was the mood of the day.

The party went on all afternoon into the night, an open house. Small children were playing underfoot and it was easier to pay attention to them, to talk about them.

There was a pulped concoction in the middle of the table we could not define or describe. Meaty, but it wasn't meat. Eggplant one of our best friends said. She was trying out a new recipe that day and wanted everyone's opinion. Soon we would be gone and they'd be eating it without us at the next dinner party. Would they keep empty chairs for us like Elijah?

We had thoughts we couldn't share even with each other. A plan was the safest way to express change: what time we had to leave in the morning, what time the plane would land, who would pick us up.

Years later, we remembered this party—what we'd saved, what we'd given away. And though there was only so much we could ship and carry, we knew it had been a mistake to give away our possessions before we were ready.

CONSIDERING FURNITURE

In early summer the servants covered the furniture with white sheets and packed our bags—well, the bags got packed first—and emptied the refrigerator and our mother instructed them—the servants—to have a good summer, take some time off, go to the beach, play with their children. It was up to them to lock up, shut down all the windows, turn off the lights, she told them. Because we trust you, our father said. And depend upon you, our mother said.

We waved goodbye from the back seat of our new car: two adults, two children, my brother and me. Goodbye, we waved. Goodbye. We had a chauffeur in those days, too.

That summer in Newport was like all the others. Long mornings reading on the veranda, playdates with friends, sand castles on the beach. I wasn't interested in boys yet but my brother had a girlfriend down the street and we saw very little of him. My mother didn't seem to mind. She had her own preoccupations. Our father was either playing golf, or reading, or talking to his broker on the phone.

Labor Day came and we packed and the Newport servants cleaned the house and covered the furniture with white sheets and we clambered into the back seat of the car and headed back to the city. When we arrived at the apartment sheets were still on the furniture, the house was empty of servants and smelled of smoke. Our parents were silent; they never showed much emotion. There'd been a fire in the building next door and they hadn't heard a word. All our furniture was ruined.

PERFECT WEATHER

We've been waiting for perfect weather. It's finally arrived. The sun is out, the temperature is temperate, there's no prospect of rain in the hours ahead, and though the word "cloudy" is in the forecast, we've decided to risk a journey to the seashore to collect shells and soak in some sun after a long, hard, endless winter. Of course, it wasn't really endless because here we are and the weather is perfect today, it's spring at last. And if we continue to postpone our outing to the seashore, it will never happen, will it? We can't rely on the weather or plan around the weather all the time especially if the forecast is uncertain, as it often is. But that is exactly what we've been doing lately—postponing and postponing and postponing.

From time to time I have imagined a solution to our weather problem: we could move. If we moved to another city in another state, or even a city in another country, the weather problem we have where we live now would not exist.

THE POET

The well-known poet got up onto the stage to read his work. There was a large audience, his fans filled the room. He brought the microphone very close to his mouth. His words were percussive, angry. Yet he was reciting—more like declaiming—a seasonal poem.

Months earlier, when I had been arranging the schedule of events at the café, I had asked the well-known poet if he would agree to share the evening with a younger, less established poet. He had agreed. At the time, I hadn't picked up on his reluctance. Unlike his work, it was subtle, or maybe I didn't know him very well, or at all, for that matter. I only knew his work—which I liked—and his reputation as a gadfly, which had nothing to do with me. I am not a poet, I am the manager of a café. I suppose he understood that if he refused, I would not put him on the schedule, he'd have to find another venue.

The trouble started two weeks before the reading. I invited him to a rehearsal —we wanted to time the reading— and he didn't get back to me for several days. When he finally did call, he said he'd have to ask his wife. He wasn't married so I laughed. "I don't need a rehearsal," he said. "I'm good at timing myself and I like to decide on the spot what I will read. I feel the mood in the room."

Meanwhile, the young, less-established poet, was getting more and more nervous. And so was I because I'd invited the press.

He stayed on the stage for a very long time, well beyond his limit, which was twenty minutes, long enough for any poet. On and on he went, spitting and declaiming into the microphone. People were holding their ears, people were walking out. I wish I could have done the same.

Salamanders
In My Pockets

DOGS WELCOME

A friend from college is getting married. Children are not invited to the wedding. It's on Long Island, a real bitch to get to, not that she considered anyone's travel challenges when she booked the venue. "They allow dogs," she told me. What does that mean? Dogs are invited but children aren't? That's a paraphrase of my impatient question. Why can't this high-powered lawyer friend of mine connect her own dots?

I don't want to go, my husband doesn't want to go, my daughter wouldn't have cared less if I'd mentioned it to her, which I didn't. The question is: should I boycott this wedding, insult my friend, and probably say sayonara to the friendship.

In the end what does it all matter? The other day on 60 minutes, one of my favorite programs, Michael Caine, who had just turned 82, said: "I don't know how I got here." That was a sad statement. Had he been sleeping all his life?

My friend is like that, too. She doesn't know how she got anywhere.

So I've made a decision: I will leave my husband and daughter behind and go to the wedding with our dog. After all, dogs are welcome.

THE $5,000 NECKLACE

There was no emotion attached to the revelation: the necklace was missing. We were walking on the street side-by-side. Her face was in profile, the street crowded and noisy. Had I misunderstood? "I thought it would turn up again as I was packing for this move," she said.

"You owned a necklace worth $5,000?"

"Yes, I bought it as a present for myself in Paris."

As friendships go, I had known this woman for a long time. She always dressed modestly: good fabrics, conventional cuts, no loud colors. Her taste in entertainment and books was the same. Nothing out of the ordinary. Early to bed, early to rise, nothing unexpected at work or play. But she was single—no partner of either gender for all the years I'd known her, no dating that she talked about. And all her friends, including me, had wondered about her reclusiveness. "What explains our friend's odd life?" we whispered to each other in our more gossipy moods.

"Did you lose it or was it stolen?" I asked.

"I don't know."

"Was it insured?"

"No."

There were now three announcements to process: the necklace itself, its loss, and the fact that it hadn't been insured.

"This is unprecedented," I said. "I did not realize..."

We had arrived at the subway station, said goodnight, and went our separate ways to different trains. She would be leaving the city for good in a few days. And that did not seem to matter to her either.

DOPPLEGANGER

A woman approached me on the pool deck. "Hi, Jan. It's good to see you. We missed you in class today."

She was an instructor I have seen working in the warm, small pool for babies and "the elderly" many times. Her particular class is for women of a certain age who have stiff joints. She plays loud, funky music and was toting her boom box. Class was over and I'd missed it!

I may be a woman of a certain age, but I am a lap swimmer who once upon a time was a competitive swimmer. And my joints may be stiff, but I pay no attention. I don't take classes and I had never talked to this instructor before.

So her approach to me was weird. "I don't take any classes," I told her.

That startled her. "Oh my, and your name is Jan? You have a Doppelgänger. Another Jan, similar build."

I didn't like this story, it made me uncomfortable. Not only did this Doppelgänger look like me, she had the same name.

I don't want a "twin" who is unrelated. But I was also intrigued, albeit eerily so. In mythology—German, Norse, Egyptian—a Doppelgänger is an evil twin and harbinger of bad luck or death. No thank you.

I stuck with my intuition and didn't take my inquiry further. I got into the pool and had a good swim.

DR. PHIL, MY INNER CHILD AND ME

Dr. Phil recommends that we take care of our inner child so I have decided to bring her with me to his show. A friend gave me free tickets. I am very excited to see this great man in person. I am hoping that if I raise my hand, he will call on me.

My inner child is wearing a light blue dress with long sleeves. Her dark black hair is curly and thick. She's three-years-old and very talkative.

The topic of today's show is obedience and defying authority. That's complicated for a three-year-old so I plan to interpret as Dr. Phil speaks.

I settle into my seat and put my inner child on my lap. No one sees her, of course, but I know she is there. She is heavy and fidgety. I ask her to calm down but she doesn't calm down.

Two grownups are on the stage talking about their disobedient children. They seem mean and impatient just like my parents. I disobeyed them and left home when I was sixteen. I never finished high school and now I have a low-level job and an inner child to take care of. It's no fun.

I raise my hand and Dr. Phil calls on me. I like his voice. He's handsome in person and he's tall, very tall. He stands up when he talks to me. I ask a question and he is kind when he answers. He praises my concern for my inner child who is very disobedient. He suggests I come backstage and talk to him after the show. I'm thrilled. Maybe he'll give me his autograph.

I AM OFFERED A PRODUCT

"All I want to do is deposit this check," I tell the young man whose name is Louis, according to the label on his wrinkled white shirt.

"Today is your lucky day because the bank is offering a special product. And you have been pre-approved, your credit is good," Louis says.

I've arrived at an off-hour, my intention, I hate lines and waiting, and here I am waylaid by a sales pitch by Louis, the teller, who I had thought was employed to take my deposit, hand me cash, or help me solve a discrepancy on my statement.

I've handed him my check with the deposit slip but he still hasn't processed it. I look at my watch. Three minutes.

He's very friendly, has a sweet face and he's young, so I am trying to be patient. Five minutes.

"Louis, listen, I'm not here to purchase anything, I'm here to deposit a check. It's a simple transaction."

"This is a really good deal. If you spend $500 in a month you get $200 back."

"How does that work?"

I've asked a question. Big mistake.

Seven minutes.

"Look I can fill out this form, right here, right now."

"Sure, do it, Louis. Let's be done with this. I'm hungry. I need to get some lunch. Do me a favor and tell your boss that you are no longer a teller, you're a salesman. And a good one."

THE DALAI LAMA IS A FRIEND OF MINE

And have I mentioned that I meet him in the locker room at the gym. Of course he is never alone; he has an entourage. He enters in his saffron robes but discards them. He chats easily. He smiles. He guffaws.

His doctors—more than one—have suggested a regimen and he must obey (guffaw). He is handed shorts and a tank top. He is fleshy I notice, his muscles are flaccid. "I see you are well formed," he says.

"I work-out a lot," I reply.

"And how do you find it?"

"Congenial," I reply.

Now he chortles—a lighter laugh than a guffaw—and sits down on the bench to put on exercise shorts on top of his boxer shorts. (Yes, the Dalai Lama wears boxer shorts.)

"And now the tank top," he says. "We had a wonderful shopping spree in Modell's."

He leans over me and puts his hand on my bare shoulder. It is calloused, which surprises me. I have always thought of the Dalai Lama as a baby, like Jesus in the manger. But he is a grown fleshy man, a mere mortal, like me.

THE SEVEN FOOT MAN
WITH THE SMALL HEAD

The seven foot man with the small head came into the locker room. I wasn't sure at first if he was a potato with a stalk or a person. But then another reporter arrived and he introduced me to the seven foot man. He said, "I think the two of you will have a lot in common. The only problem is, I don't know how old he is."

I decided to ask as soon as we were introduced. "How old are you?"

"Four, the big man said."

The locker room was a *cul de sac,* too small for a seven foot man trying to put on his street clothes after a game. His limbs stretched from one end of the bench to the other. Reporters were crowded all around him. He'd made a lot of baskets and won the game for his team.

I wasn't interested in all of that. I wanted to go out with him. I was the only female reporter in the room. Lucky me! And I liked the seven foot man with the small head. He was jolly and friendly.

I asked him if he'd like to go out for a drink. He said, sure, at least I think that is what he said. His head was too far away for me to hear him clearly, as small and as distant as a galaxy in another universe.

YOU SHOULD NOT PUSH
THE ELEVATOR BUTTON

Because you have entered the elevator, quite naturally you want to push the button. You do not think for a minute that the two other people in the elevator have already pushed the button. Note: you are all going down to the lobby. Now there are three people who have pushed the L button.

Because no one is talking there is no communication about buttons or where the elevator is going because, obviously, it is going down. Perhaps no one trusts that the button is working, or that the elevator is, in fact, going down, or that it will arrive safely.

At first, when you began to notice this quirk in every human who enters the elevator, you assumed it was only office workers in very tall buildings who pushed the L button. But even in your small, friendly building, everyone pushes the L button. First they say hello or good morning and then they push the button even though they know, as you know, that someone who has entered the elevator before them has pushed the button. You seem relieved when a dog enters the elevator. Dogs do not push buttons though, undoubtedly, they trust their owners to push it for them.

OTHER PEOPLE'S DREAMS

"I had a very interesting dream last night," he says.

All the chatter stops, we must be polite, he is our host, we are captive.

Has he gathered us for the very purpose of reciting his dream? Would he like to hear ours? Does he expect commentary? Interpretation? Once I tried to recite my own dream but he cut me off and asked if anyone would like some dessert.

NARCISSISM: SOME EXAMPLES

Instead of asking, how are you doing, you tell me how you are doing.

Instead of asking, how are your spirits after your difficult year—we haven't seen each other in a year—you begin a recitation of all your recent travels, your daughter's engagement, and the brilliance of your new boyfriend. I think "dogged" is the word you use to describe him, meaning that he can solve any problem, and does.

Instead of asking, what can I do for you as a friend right now, you complain about a mutual friend's snarky comment to which I cannot respond without being disloyal. But that is the point: you want me to be disloyal to her and loyal only to you.

Instead of complimenting me on my strength, you tell me about a dear friend with Parkinson's who is stronger than anyone you know, mostly because of your ministrations, for which he is eternally grateful.

Oddly, you ask about my husband. Do I have a recent picture? Whereupon you pull out your iPhone to show me pictures of your new boyfriend, your new condo in New Orleans, and your daughter's handsome fiancé.

Instead of asking how my daughter is doing, you ask about her hair. Is it long or short? Then you tell me about your new hair stylist.

Finally, you ask about a concert I played the other night which you could not attend because you were attending to yourself. How did it go? Whereupon you pull out a DVD of a recital you played in Venice. Would I like a copy, you ask, as you hand it to me. Although it was many years ago, you have not forgotten the applause.

AT THE NAIL SALON

I decided to get a pedicure. My nails were very long, it was summer, time for sandals. My wife said, "They are disgusting, you are piercing my shins in bed, how do you expect me to play footsie with you?"

I had been to my wife's preferred nail salon once before when we went for an anniversary his/her manicure/pedicure. We sat next to each other and vibrated our chairs. We chatted to the workers: mine was from Ecuador, hers was from China. "How long have you been here?" is the usual opening question. Usually, they don't understand or pretend not to understand. Mostly, they're illegal, we get that, but chatting passes the time. Also, enjoying the knee-ankle massage, the vibrating chair, browsing through women's magazines, or checking email.

This time, I had my wife's Chinese worker. She was wearing a jade bracelet on one arm and either a Fitbit or an Apple watch on the other. Maybe she owned the salon, I thought, because these watches are expensive. I wanted to clarify the kind of watch and her relationship to the salon. I wanted her to notice me. I'd heard her talking in English as well as Chinese. She was completely bi-lingual, maybe even born in New York.

"Is that a Fitbit or an Apple watch?" I asked. Then I pointed to the less expensive Fitbit on my arm.

"What do you think of it?" I continued.

She hadn't been looking at me or my disgusting feet; she'd been looking up, around, talking in Chinese to a compadre. Now she looked at me. It was a look of disdain: how dare I interrupt her private reverie or inquire about her watch? She dropped my left foot back into the water and walked away. Five minutes later, another woman took her place.

"Where are you from originally?" I began.

"No understand English," was the reply.

PREFACE TO THE CLOUDSPOTTER'S
GUIDE TO THE UNIVERSE

If you've loved looking at clouds, this book is for you. And if you've never noticed clouds, perhaps this book will inspire you to do so.

A few years ago I decided to look at clouds in a new way. I went to the park and sat on a bench for about an hour. I studied the river, the trees, the flowers, the boats on the river, and the leaves on the trees. Then I looked up. After a while I couldn't see anything but the sky and the clouds. I took out my iPhone and snapped some pictures. Clouds are very photogenic.

I don't worry about remembering their Latin names: cumulus, cirrocumulus, lenticularis, etc. These were invented by professional cloud spotters and scientists. I am an amateur.

Where does a cloud begin and where does it end? Where does it come from and where does it go? Did cave men and cave women tell stories about clouds? When did they first appear in our atmosphere? Do all the planets—those we know about and those still unknown—have clouds in their atmosphere?

Arriving at these questions is like learning a new song. So let's sing it.

ACKNOWLEDGMENTS

The author wishes to thank her beloved and loving husband, Jim Bergman, for his time, his expertise, his patience and his encouragement.

The author wishes to thank her beloved and exceptional daughter, Chloe Annetts, for her time, her expertise, her patience and her encouragement.

To all my friends, family and students, thank you for sustaining this writer in her modest efforts.

AN INTERVIEW WITH
THE AUTHOR

Q: I'd like to discuss the entire NOMADS trilogy if you don't mind. How did you begin? Is it finished?

A: I began in 2000 when I was working on "Another Day in Paradise," a book about international humanitarian workers. I compiled, edited the book, and ghosted some of the stories. It took two years and it was engrossing, very intense. I had to travel a bit and work with many stories about war, atrocities and natural disasters. In order to keep myself grounded while working on the "Another Day" project, I began to sketch small stories. It was all I had time to do for myself in between the traveling, interviewing and editing.

Q: Why did you decide to collect these stories and publish them?

A: I showed a few to writer friends and they commented on the precision of the writing, the unusual genre I'd chosen (similar to Lydia Davis, they said), and the experimental feel of the work—not fact, not fiction, something new and different for me—as I either write journalism, blogs, or dedicated fiction. So I decided to write more short short stories and see what happened. It was an exploration, a writing discipline. What is fact and what is fiction? Do we always have to disclaim when we are not writing journalism? My view is that if we mess with the facts we are creating factoids (a Norman Mailer word) and therefore we are totally in the realm of fiction. I certainly tell my nonfiction students to be careful—not to conflate or fabricate. NOMADS are fictions and understanding that, accepting it, gave me freedom.

Titles began to accumulate in my journal. Before long I had enough pieces for the first volume.

Q: Why did you decide to use actors for the launch of each NOMADS book at the Cornelia Street Café?

A: It happened serendipitously. I reconnected with my daughter's long-ago babysitter, Stephanie Stone. She's an actor. I had moved into Stephanie's neighborhood and we would walk and talk on Saturday mornings. She invited me to a poetry reading—all actors reading well-known poems. The actors' expression evoked new interpretations. And, of course, they are articulate and can project. So I said to Stephanie, "What if I had a launch and I sat in the audience and you read my work?" We rehearsed an evening for the first NOMADS with two other actor/directors: Constance George and Burke Walker. I am grateful to all of them. They told me that many of the stories read like monologues. Some even have dialogue and were read by two of the actors. Most importantly, to hear my work read and re-interpreted by the actors was an exciting experience for me. It changed the way I wrote the pieces for Nomads 2 and Nomads 3. I sometimes hear them "spoken." I'd taken a playwriting class—and failed dismally. The actors did well but I didn't; my instinct is always to write narrative prose. I came up with ideas but couldn't get anything to work using dialogue. Now I think the class did have a delayed effect. Maybe I'll eventually be able to write a "play." I think Richard Caliban, my playwriting teacher at Gotham Writers Workshop, would be pleased.

Q. Is the NOMADS series finished?

A. I think it is—mostly—because I want to get on to other things. And once I have that desire, I know I am done. Most writers move into new projects with ease; we rarely look back. And though I am calling NOMADS a trilogy because I wrote each book over time, my sense is that it is all one work, and that it is finished.

"Sit finis libri, non finis quaerendi."

(Here ends the book, but not the searching.)

--Thomas Merton

* 9 7 8 0 6 1 5 9 2 4 0 2 1 *